THE ULTIMATE
UNAUTHORIZED
STEPHEN KING
TRIVIA CHALLENGE

THE ULTIMATE UNAUTHORIZED STEPHEN KING
TRIVIA CHALLENGE

HUNDREDS OF BRAINTEASING QUESTIONS
ON MINUTE DETAILS AND LITTLE-KNOWN
FACTS ABOUT THE WORLD'S LEADING
HORROR WRITER AND HIS WORK

ROBERT W. BLY

Kensington Books
http://www.kensingtonbooks.com

813.54

BLY

KENSINGTON BOOKS are published by

Kensington Publishing Corp.
850 Third Avenue
New York, NY 10022

ISBN 1-57566-228-0

First Kensington Trade Paperback Printing: November, 1997
10 9 8 7 6 5 4 3 2 1

Printed in the United States of America

To Fern Dickey and Mildred Bly
—my favorite Stephen King fans

ACKNOWLEDGMENTS

Thanks to Tony Seidl and Paul Dinas, for making *The Ultimate Unauthorized Stephen King Trivia Challenge* reality. And to Stephen King, for many pleasurable hours of reading.

CONTENTS

PART TWO: THE BACHMAN BOOKS

PART THREE: THE SHORT STORIES

PART FOUR: MOVIES AND TV

PART FIVE: STEPHEN KING, UP CLOSE AND PERSONAL

PART SIX: ANSWER KEY

PREFACE

With more than 150 million books sold, Stephen King is one of the most popular authors of all time. His movies gross in the tens of millions of dollars per picture. His TV miniseries often get the major share of the viewing market and are typically broadcast during sweeps week.

Other writers have readers; Stephen King has *fans*. More than a dozen books have been written about King and his work. He is mobbed whenever he speaks at conventions. There was even a Stephen King newsletter at one point, with a circulation in the tens of thousands. His books are so popular, there is a book club that sells *only* Stephen King books. First editions of his novels have fetched over $2000 at auction.

The Ultimate Unauthorized Stephen King Trivia Challenge taps into the King-mania market. It appeals to the legions of King fans who buy everything they can get their hands on by . . . and about . . . their favorite writer. I wrote it for a simple reason: I love Stephen King's books and this is the kind of quiz book I could have fun with. Searching your memory for answers to these questions will put your Stephen King knowledge to the test . . . and bring back memories of many happy hours spent lost in his fantasies.

The book is divided into five major sections: the novels, the Bachman books (books King wrote under the pseudonym Richard Bachman), short stories, movies and TV, and King's personal and professional life. The questions are tricky enough to challenge you and give you a mental workout, but not so esoteric that they frustrate you. It's trivia, it's Stephen King, and it's fun. Enjoy!

PART ONE

THE NOVELS

CARRIE

1. What special power did Carrie possess?

2. What substance was dumped on Carrie by pranksters at the prom?

3. How long did it take Stephen King to write the first draft of *Carrie?*

4. In what fictional town does Carrie live?

5. Where did King's wife, Tabitha, find the manuscript for *Carrie* when she first read it and encouraged King to finish the novel?

6. How long is the novel *Carrie?*

7. What publisher put out *Carrie* in hardcover? How much of an advance did they pay for the book?

8. What publisher put out *Carrie* in paperback? How much of an advance did they pay for the book?

9. What were the names of the three unpublished novels King wrote before *Carrie* was published?

10. Who was King's editor for *Carrie*?

11. Which of the following bands played at the Ewen High School Senior Prom?
    (a) Speed Racer and the Jets
    (b) The Billy Bosnan Band
    (c) Josie and the Moonglows
    (d) The Beat Street Rejects
    (e) Castle Rock Rockers

12. What material was Carrie's prom dress made of?

13. At what time did the whistle atop the town hall on Main Street begin to shriek on the night of the prom?

14. How many people were killed by Carrie White's attack on prom night?
    (a) 4
    (b) 14
    (c) 44
    (d) 440
    (e) none

15. Who rigged the bucket for Carrie's "Prom Queen Shower"? What kind of car did he drive?

16. Who took Carrie White to the prom?

17. What type of record player did Margaret White own?

18. What did Margaret White do when Carrie told her she wanted to attend the prom?

19. Where did Roger Fearon work?

20. To what hospital was Margaret White admitted for a suspected out-of-wedlock miscarriage on April 3, 1962?

'SALEM'S LOT

1. What bad thing happens to good people in 'Salem's Lot?

2. How long did it take King to write *'Salem's Lot?*

3. How many copies of *'Salem's Lot* were sold?

4. Who is Larry Crockett's silent partner in the supermarket plaza deal?

5. Of what firm was Hubert Marsten president?

6. What is the name of the master vampire in 'Salem's Lot? What is the name of his business partner and human emissary?

7. In 'Salem's Lot, what phone number do you dial to call an ambulance?

8. For how much money does Susan Norton sell a dozen of her paintings to the Cinex Corporation?

(a) $70
(b) $700
(c) $1700
(d) $7000
(e) $70,000

9. How much of an advance does Ben Mears get from Random House for his novel?
   (a) $1200
   (b) $6000
   (c) $12,000
   (d) $120,000
   (e) $1.2 million

10. How much money was Larry Crockett asking for the hilltop house he was selling on Taggart Stream Road?

11. Where does Susan Norton have her hair done?

12. What is the title of Ben Mears's published novel?

13. How much did Judge Hooker fine Horace Kilby's son for smoking dope?

14. Where in 'Salem's Lot does Ben Mears start a brushfire with a cigarette?

15. What corporation owned the land on which Straker and Barlow's Portland shopping center was to be built?

16. What brand of ham do the Broddins eat?

17. On whose tombstone are the words, "God Grant He Lie Still"?

18. With whom does Bonnie Sawyer have an extramarital affair?

19. Which of these publications did Hubert Marsten subscribe to?
    (a) *The Saturday Evening Post*
    (b) *The New Yorker*
    (c) *Amazing Stories*
    (d) *The Magazine of Fantasy and Science Fiction*
    (e) *The Wall Street Journal*
    (f) *The Commodities Journal*

20. Who is the priest at St. Andrews? How does he die?

THE SHINING

1. At what hotel is Jack Torrance hired to be caretaker during the off-season?

2. What is the significance of the word "redrum" that Danny chants?

3. How many copies of *The Shining* were sold?

4. What happens to the hotel when it is leased in 1961 by four writers?

5. What radio station do the Torrances listen to while they are caretakers of the hotel?

6. How many rooms are in the hotel?
   (a) 10
   (b) 50
   (c) 110
   (d) 120
   (e) 150

7. Who hired Jack Torrance as caretaker?

8. How old is Danny Torrance? How old is Dick Hallorann?

9. Where did George Hatfield go to school?

10. What drink does Jack Torrance order from Jack the Bartender?
    (a) whiskey sour
    (b) manhattan
    (c) gin and tonic
    (d) martini
    (e) boilermaker
    (f) rum and coke

11. When is the hotel open for business?

12. What kind of gun does Jack Torrance own?

13. Which of these credit cards did the hotel accept?
    (a) MasterCharge
    (b) American Express
    (c) Bank Americard
    (d) Discovery Card
    (e) Visa

14. What is the room number of the hotel's Presidential Suite?

15. With whom did Marilyn Monroe once stay at the hotel?

16. Of what pinball machine company is Richard Scarne the principal stockholder?

17. What is Dick Hallorann's term for the mental powers he and Danny Torrance possess?

18. What is Vito Gienelli's nickname? Why is he called this?

19. In what year was Peter Zeiss convicted on charges of receiving and concealing stolen property?
    (a) 1957
    (b) 1958
    (c) 1959
    (d) 1960
    (e) 1961

THE STAND

1. What disease wipes out more than 90 percent of the Earth's population?
   (a) a mutated AIDS virus
   (b) radiation from nuclear waste
   (c) the super-flu
   (d) cancer
   (e) the black death

2. Who is the Dark Man?

3. What is the name of the ten-year-old Maine girl who falls off her bike and dies of a fractured skull?

4. What does Eileen Drummond drink a whole bottle of in order to get drunk?

5. According to the Law Committee, how many adults sit on the tribunal?

6. Under what Defense Department contract was the "sniffer" manufactured?

7. How old is Mother Abigail?

8. What is the slang name for the disease that wipes out most of humanity?

9. What is the Trashcan Man's real name?

10. What type of guitar does Leo take from the Earthly Sounds music store?

11. What is the name of the guinea pig used to determine that Stu Redman was immune to the disease?

12. In which town park does Frannie Goldsmith throw stones in the duck pond after Gus Dinsmore dies?

13. How many words were added to *The Stand* when Doubleday published the "complete and uncut" version in 1990?
    (a) 25,000
    (b) 50,000
    (c) 100,000
    (d) 150,000
    (e) 250,000

14. What is the name of Glen Bateman's dog?
    (a) Serpico
    (b) Columbo
    (c) Baretta
    (d) Kojak
    (e) Spencer

15. Where and when was Nick Andros born?

16. When Randall Flagg is reborn, what name does he use?

17. What is the code name of the secret government project designed to stop the spread of the disease?

18. Who invents a doorbell that could be rung by a walkie-talkie from a distance?

19. Which of the following are members of the Free Zone Ad Hoc Committee?
    (a) Nick Andros
    (b) Glen Bateman
    (c) Fran Goldsmith
    (d) Susan Stern
    (e) Ralph Brentner

20. What song does Tim Cullen sing after he opens his Christmas gifts from Stu?

THE DEAD ZONE

1. For how long is Johnny Smith in a coma?

2. In the dedication to *The Dead Zone,* by what nickname does Stephen King call his son, Owen King?

3. How much money does Greg Stillson earn in 1975?
   (a) $26,000
   (b) $36,000
   (c) $46,000
   (d) $56,000
   (e) $66,000

4. Where does Johnny Smith have an ice-skating accident in 1953?

5. What did presidential candidate Greg Stillson do for a living in 1953, the year Johnnie had his skating accident?

6. How does murderer Frank Dodd, the Castle Rock Strangler, die?

7. On what date does Johnny awaken from his coma?

8. What type of rifle does Johnny use in his attempted assassination of Greg Stillson?

9. What is the classical radio station in Mount Washington?

10. How much money is the vial of water, drawn from the springs at Lourdes, that Vera Smith wants to order from a mail-order catalog?

11. How many milligrams of valium does Dr. Brown order for John Smith to calm him down?

12. What type of car does Roger Chatsworth drive?

13. Who does *Newsweek* call "The New Hurkos"?

14. How old is Greg Stillson when he runs for president?

15. Under whom did Hector Markstone serve in World War I?

16. What does Elton Curry do for a living?

17. To what comic does Roger Chatsworth compare Greg Stillson?
    (a) Jerry Seinfeld
    (b) George Carlin
    (c) Chevy Chase
    (d) Carrot Top
    (e) Milton Berle

18. Where does Arnie Tremont work as a mechanic?

19. What is the "Dead Zone"?

20. What supermarket tabloid offers John Smith a job as
    a psychic?
    (a) *The National Enquirer*
    (c) *The Star*
    (c) *Inside View Magazine*
    (d) *World Weekly*
    (e) *National Reporter*

6

FIRESTARTER

1. What sinister government agency wants to exploit Charlie McGee's special powers?
   (a) the CIA
   (b) the FBI
   (c) StarLabs
   (d) the Shop
   (e) the A Team

2. What experimental drug gives Andy McGee a partial ability to control men's minds?

3. How much was Andy paid to participate in this experiment?
   (a) $100
   (b) $200
   (c) $300
   (d) $400
   (e) $500

4. What mental power does Charlie McGee possess? What is her name for it?

5. What is Charlie's mother's maiden name?

6. Where do Charlie and Andy go after Manders farm burns down?

7. What is John Rainbird obsessed with?

8. What is Dr. Herman Pynchot's IQ?
   (a) 125
   (b) 135
   (c) 145
   (d) 155
   (e) 165

9. To what magazine does Charlie McGee give the story of the Shop and the Lot Six experiment and its aftermath?
   (a) *The New York Times*
   (b) *The Boston Globe*
   (c) *Newsweek*
   (d) *U.S. News & World Report*
   (e) *Rolling Stone*

10. Who runs the U.S. Bureau for Geological Understudies?

11. What power does Vickie McGee have? What other Stephen King character had it?

12. Where are Vickie and Andy given experimental drug doses in a government research project?

13. In *Firestarter*, what is the full name of the character known as O.J. or "The Juice"?

14. What is Cap Hollister's code name for access to the government computing system?

15. What political disease did Cap think Nixon suffered from?

16. For what corporation does James Richardson work?

17. Where did Andy McGee bank?
    (a) Chase Manhattan
    (b) Chemical Allied Bank
    (c) Citibank
    (d) First National Community Bank
    (e) Durham National Bank

18. What was the name of Granther McGee's dog?

19. Who was "The Mad Doctor"?

20. What type of car did Andy McGee tell the desk clerk at the Slumberland Hotel he was driving? What license number did he give?

CUJO

1. What kind of dog is Cujo?
   (a) German shepherd
   (b) Saint Bernard
   (c) collie
   (d) pit bull
   (e) rottweiler
   (f) Doberman pinscher

2. What is the name of Vic Trenton's advertising agency?

3. What is Tad Trenton's favorite cereal? Who makes it?

4. Who is Vic Trenton's mechanic and Cujo's owner?

5. In what kind of car are Tad and Donna Trenton trapped by Cujo?

6. What Sharp cereal has major publicity problems when it turns milk red?

7. How old is Cujo? How much does he weigh?

8. Of what company is Vietnam veteran Rob Martin president?

9. What business does Alva Thornton own?

10. What does Donna Trenton do to Cujo after he dies?

11. Who is the biggest employer in Castle Rock, Maine?

12. True or false?—In the novel *Cujo*, Tad Trenton dies at the end.

13. What is Vic's nickname for Tad?

14. Who is Joe Cambers's mailman? What is his medical problem?

15. With whom does Donna Trenton have an extramarital affair?

16. What are the Monster Words?

17. What is the first account Vic and Roger get for the Ellison agency?

18. What brand of maple syrup does Donna Trent pour on her waffles?

19. Who is Tad's favorite *Star Wars* character?
    (a) Han Solo
    (b) Yoda
    (c) Greedo
    (d) Jaba the Hut
    (e) Darth Vader

20. To whom did Stephen Kind dedicate *Cujo*?

THE DARK TOWER I:
THE GUNSLINGER

1. Who illustrated *The Dark Tower I: The Gunslinger?*

2. What is the first line of *The Dark Tower?*

3. Where, in magazine form, were the stories that make up *The Gunslinger* originally published?

4. What discipline does Roland practice to gain control over his mind and body?

5. What precious resource does the Gunslinger have a limited supply of that, once used up, cannot be replaced in his world?

6. What was the name of the hawk Roland used to defeat Cort?

7. What metal are Roland's guns forged from?

8. What kind of weed grows in the Mohaine desert?

9. What kind of car kills Jake Chambers on Earth?

10. What mutated creatures try to trap Roland and Jake in their cave?

11. What do boys lust for "more than power or riches or women"?

12. What has happened to Roland when he awakens from his sleep at the campfire where he and the Man in Black have met?

13. Who is the keeper of the Tower?

14. Who lives backwards in time?

15. What is glammer?

16. When Jake's father was stopped for speeding on the New Jersey Turnpike, how fast was he going?
    (a) 69 mph
    (b) 75 mph
    (c) 85 mph
    (d) 99 mph
    (e) 100 mph

17. Which of the following was Jake carrying in his lunch bag on the day he was killed?
    (a) a salami sandwich
    (b) a bologna sandwich
    (c) a peanut butter and jelly sandwich
    (d) a banana
    (e) Oreo cookies
    (f) Fig Newtons

18. What is the Man in Black's real name?

19. What is the raven's name?

20. What does the Gunslinger order for lunch at Sheb's?

9

CHRISTINE

1. What model car is Christine?
   (a) 1957 Pontiac Indian Chief
   (b) 1958 Chevrolet Impala
   (c) 1958 Plymouth Fury
   (d) 1968 Mustang convertible
   (e) 1961 Mercedes Benz

2. How much did Arnie Cunningham pay Roland D. LeBay for Christine?
   (a) $25
   (b) $100
   (c) $250
   (d) $500
   (e) $750

3. For what firm did Arnie Cunningham and Dennis Guilder work on the road crew during the summer? On what stretch of road did they work?

4. Where does Dennis take Roseanne dancing?

5. Who taught Dennis and Arnie in their "Topics in American History" class?

6. How tall is Leigh Cabot?

7. What was the name of Dennis's pet cat? How was he killed?

8. Where does Arnie garage and work on Christine?

9. Who fell through the ice on Palmer Pond and drowned?

10. Who is killed by a car, made from "haunted" scrap metal, at a drive-in movie theater in L.A.?

11. What kind of car does Dennis Guilder drive?

12. What Maine radio station plays mostly oldies?

13. To what horror movie director is *Christine* dedicated?

14. What does "A.B." stand for?

15. What is the title of the book being written by Dennis Guilder's mother?

16. Against what team is Dennis Guilder playing when he has an accident that breaks both his legs?

17. What kind of car does Buddy Repperton drive?

18. When Arnie bought Christine, how many miles did she have on her?

19. What was the original name of JFK Drive?

20. What company employs Kenny Guilder, Dennis's dad, as a tax consultant?

PET SEMATARY

1. What does Louis Creed do for a living?

2. What mythological beast is said to roam the woods of Canada and the Northern United States?

3. How old was Louis Creed when his father passed away?
   (a) 3
   (b) 13
   (c) 20
   (d) 30
   (e) 33

4. What is the name of the cat Louis Creed buries in the Pet Sematary?

5. What happens to Louis's son Gage after Louis buries him in the Pet Sematary?

6. How many acres did the Micmac Indian tribe own in Ludlow, Maine?

7. What type of house do the Creeds move into when they relocate to Ludlow?

8. Who is Louis Creed's closest neighbor in Ludlow? How old is he?

9. What disease does Norma Crandall suffer from?

10. What game is Louis Creed playing when his wife comes back from the dead?

11. Who tells Louis Creed, "The soil of a man's heart is stonier"?

12. What is Louis Creed's annual salary?

13. When was Trixie killed on the highway?

14. With whom does Louis have a fistfight at Gage's funeral?

15. What is the name of the Indian doctor on Louis Creed's staff?

16. Who is Louis Creed's physician's assistant?

17. In what magazine does Louis Creed get his articles published?

18. As a hobby, Louis Creed was assembling a model car with 680 pieces, including over 50 moving parts. What kind of car was it?

19. What kind of car does Louis Creed drive to and from work?

20. What kind of camera does Rachel have?

CYCLE OF THE WEREWOLF

1. What are the titles of the twelve chapters in *Cycle of the Werewolf*?

2. How many victims did the werewolf kill? How frequently did he kill?

3. How many members are there in Reverend Lowe's congregation?
   (a) 25
   (b) 50
   (c) 100
   (d) 200
   (e) 300
   (f) 500

4. What was Arnie Westrum's job?

5. How did the werewolf kill Milt Sturmfuller, the Tarker's Mills town librarian?

6. Who shoots and kills the werewolf with two silver bullets, despite being confined to a wheelchair?

7. How did the werewolf kill Arnie Knopfler?

8. Stella Randolph believes she has received Valentine's Day cards from which of the following celebrities?
(a) Ace Frehy from KISS
(b) Robert Redford
(c) Frank Sinatra
(d) Clark Gable
(e) Arnold Schwarzenegger
(f) John Travolta

9. Who is the Tarker's Mills werewolf?

10. What medical disorder does Ollie Parker, the grammar school teacher, suffer from?

11. Who is the biggest drunk in Tarker's Mills?

12. What *Star Wars* character does Marty dress up as for Halloween?
(a) Darth Vader
(b) Han Solo
(c) Luke Skywalker
(d) Yoda
(e) Chewbacca

13. What did the werewolf kill at Elmer Zinneman's farm?

14. Uncle Al buys Marty which of the following types of fireworks?
(a) bottle rockets
(b) cherry bombs
(c) M-18s

(d) Roman candles

(e) Black Cat firecrackers

15. Which of the werewolf's eyes does Marty put out with a firecracker?

16. What kind of gun does Uncle Al give Marty?

17. On what hill do the children of Tarker's Mills go sledding?

18. Who is the janitor at the Grace Baptist Church? What happens to him?

19. What does Grandfather Coslaw like to drink?
    (a) tea
    (b) whiskey
    (c) buttered rum
    (d) schnapps
    (e) gin

20. Who has a crush on Reverend Lowe?

THE TALISMAN

1. With whom did Stephen King coauthor *The Talisman*?
   (a) Clive Baker
   (b) John Saul
   (c) Peter Straub
   (d) Shirley Jackson
   (e) Peter Benchley

2. Who is the "Twinner" of Jack Sawyer's mother?

3. To save his mother from terminal illness, to what lands must Jack travel?

4. How is Jack related to Morgan Sloat?

5. Where do Jack and his mother live?

6. Where is Jack attacked by animated suits of armor?

7. What is Parkus's official title in the Territories?

8. Where do Jack and Wolf stop to have Whoppers for lunch?

9. How old is Jack?

10. By what name is Jack known in the Territories?

11. Where does Gardener imprison Wolf?

12. How much money does Smokey take out of Jack's first paycheck for meals?

13. Who was the owner of the Oatley Tap?
    (a) Victor Temkin
    (b) Eddie Rabbit
    (c) Smokey Updike
    (d) George Hatfield
    (e) Robert Heidel

14. What does the Talisman look like?

15. What kind of gun does Sunlight Gardener own?

16. What does Speedy give Jack that enables him to flip into and out of the Territories at will?

17. Who starred in the feature film *Death's Darling?*

18. Which of the following foods does Albert the Blob eat?
    (a) Ring Dings
    (b) Twinkies
    (c) Famous Amos cookies
    (d) Slim Jims
    (e) Reese's Peanut Butter Cups

19. Whose spine is broken when he is run over by a cart near the Furnaces of the Black Heart?

20. What Angola, New York condominium complex is damaged by a freak earthquake?
    (a) Shady Knolls
    (b) Hidden Gardens
    (c) Eastwick Village
    (d) Rainbird Towers
    (e) The Park Chester

IT

1. Where does *It* live?

2. How many teenage children originally confront *It* in Derry, Maine?

3. Which of the following medications and vitamins does Eddie Kaspbrak take?
   (a) Serutan
   (b) One-A-Day multiple vitamins
   (c) Ex-Lax
   (d) L-Lysine
   (e) Geritol

4. Where is Christopher Philip Unwin sentenced to when convicted of second-degree manslaughter?

5. What is Bill Denbrough's speech defect?

6. What is the phone number of the Derry Town House?

7. What was Stanley Uris's starting annual salary at Corridor Video?
   (a) $20,000
   (b) $30,000
   (c) $40,000
   (d) $50,000
   (e) $65,000

8. Who is *It's* first victim?

9. Under what name does *It* appear and speak as a clown?

10. What gay man is killed when a gang of teenage boys pushes him into the Derry Canal?

11. Who does *Time* magazine call "perhaps the most promising young architect in America"?

12. On which radio station is Richard Tozier a radio personality?
    (a) WKZON
    (b) WKBRE
    (c) WPLJ
    (d) WKLAD
    (e) WABC

13. Who carved the letter "H" into Ben Hascomb's stomach with a knife?

14. What medical condition does Eddie Kaspbrak suffer from?

15. What public relations firm did Tom Rogan work for?

16. What is the title of Bill Denbrough's first published short story?

17. What message does *It* write in Jerry Bellwood's blood?

18. What is Mike Hanlon's annual income, after taxes, as Derry town librarian?

19. Under which of the following names is *It not* known?
    (a) Bob Gray
    (b) The Eater of Worlds
    (c) The Beast in the Tower
    (d) The Crawling Eye
    (e) Jaws

20. In what room at the Derry Town House did Richie Tozier stay upon his return to Derry?
    (a) 311
    (b) 404
    (c) 217
    (d) 518
    (e) 666

THE EYES OF THE DRAGON

1. Who is Old Man Spitfoot?

2. What was Stephen King's original title for *The Eyes of the Dragon?*

3. For which of his three children did King write *The Eyes of the Dragon?*

4. What is the name of the royal prison where Peter is jailed?

5. What is the name of the kingdom in which King Roland reigned?

6. What relationship is Thomas to Roland?

7. Who is the King's magician?

8. How did the Dowager Queen die?

9. Whom did King Roland marry?

10. What is the "King's Iron"?

11. What tax law did King Roland pass during the year of the great drought?

12. What is King Roland's favorite pastime?

13. What does King Roland eat the night Peter is conceived?

14. What, according to Queen Sasha, are the two natures of men?

15. How old is Peter when his mother dies?

16. What toy does Flagg think Peter is a "sissy" to play with?

17. Who kills Queen Sasha's second son when he is an infant?

18. Who is Prince Peter's best friend?

19. What title does Peter give Yosef?

20. What is the name of Peter's horse?

MISERY

1. Where does Annie live?

2. What is the name of Annie's pet pig?

3. What is the first letter that Annie's old typewriter loses?

4. What is the name of the novel Paul writes for Annie?

5. What character is the heroine of most of Paul Sheldon's novels?

6. Which manuscript of Paul's does Annie burn?

7. Which of Paul's feet does Annie cut off with an ax?

8. What station is Glenna Roberts a reporter for?

9. What does Annie call Paul when he behaves as she asks him to?

10. How does Paul Sheldon kill Annie Wilkes?

11. Who is Paul Sheldon's publisher? His editor?

12. Who is the main character in Paul Sheldon's new story about a skunk in New York City?

13. How many novels had Paul published at the time of his accident?

14. What type of condom does his father give Paul Sheldon on his fourteenth birthday?
    (a) Trojan
    (b) Mandolay
    (c) Red Devil
    (d) Deep Dragon
    (e) Tickler Deluxe

15. The livestock on Annie's farm include which of the following?
    (a) sheep
    (b) goats
    (c) cows
    (d) hens
    (e) ostriches

16. What does Annie call Paul when he uses foul language or exhibits what she considers rude or inappropriate behavior?

17. What kind of pen did Paul have in his pocket at the time of his crash?

18. Who are Annie Wilkes's nearest neighbors?

19. How old is Paul Sheldon?

20. How much in property taxes is Annie in arrears for?

THE
TOMMYKNOCKERS

1. What is buried in Roberta Anderson's back yard?
   (a) a dead body
   (b) a vampire
   (c) treasure
   (d) a spaceship
   (e) her husband, up to his neck, with a gag in his mouth
       and his tongue cut out

2. In what town does Bobbi Anderson live?

3. What did Jim Gardener give Bobbi for her birthday in 1976?

4. Who owns Burning Woods, the miles of wilderness bordering Bobbi's house at the western edge of her land?

5. How many western novels had Bobbi published when she found the Tommyknockers?
   (a) 1
   (b) 2

    (c) 5
    (d) 10
    (e) 15
    (f) 20

6. What is the title of the book of poems Bobbi published?

7. Who was the last surviving Tommyknocker?

8. What effect does the Tommyknockers' ship have on Peter?

9. What's the special at the Big Lost Weekend Bar and Grill?

10. What's Bobbi Anderson's drink?

11. What is the name of Bobbi's plumber?

12. What group is Patricia McCardle the head of?

13. What planet do the original Tommyknockers supposedly come from?

14. When Jim Gardener sticks his finger in an electrical socket, the steel plate in his head acts as a radio receiver. What does he hear over it?

15. Which of the following did Bobbi *not* grow in her garden?
    (a) beans
    (b) carrots
    (c) peas
    (d) cucumbers
    (e) radishes
    (f) cabbage

16. To what church group does John Leandro belong?

17. What prevents Gardener from examining Bobbi's water heater after she rewires it to run on D batteries?

18. Which of these dolls did Ruth McCausland have in her collection?
    (a) Russian Moss-Man
    (b) porcelain Elvis
    (c) Nixon
    (d) Glamour Barbie
    (e) Mickey Mouse

19. What type of plane does Peter Bailey own?

20. What is the main road between Derry and Haven?

THE DARK TOWER II: THE DRAWING OF THE THREE

1. What poem by Robert Browning inspired *The Dark Tower* series?

2. What does the giant lobster monster do to Roland?

3. What do the people of Roland's universe say has happened to the world?

4. What magician seduced Roland's mother while his father was away?

5. How many of Roland's 57 bullets are remaining when he awakens with his body half in the ocean?

6. Which of Roland's companions is a drug addict? What drug does he prefer?

7. What caliber are the bullets Roland's guns fire?

8. What year did Katz's Pharmacy and Soda Fountain open?

9. What medicine does Roland take to fight infection after he is attacked by the lobster monster?

10. According to Julio Estevez, what does D.R.T. stand for?

11. What gangster does Roland defeat in a gunfight? What did his men call him behind his back?

12. What year was Detta Walker born? How did she end up confined to a wheelchair?

13. What nickname does Tricks Postino give his M-16 rapid-fire assault weapon?

14. How much money is Jack Mort's Rolex watch worth?
    (a) $2500
    (b) $4500
    (c) $6500
    (d) $8500
    (e) $50

15. What words are written on the magical door Roland finds on the beach? What is there a drawing of on this door?

16. What is the name of Julio Estevez's bowling team?

17. At the end of the novel, Detta says she is three women in one. What are their names?

18. What material replaces the bone in Henry Dean's knee when he is injured in Vietnam?

19. What code came over the police radios after the shootout at Katz's Drug Store?

20. From where does Detta shoplift a $1.99 scarf?

THE DARK TOWER III: THE WASTE LANDS

1. What is the name of the intelligent robot monorail Roland, Eddie, Jake, and Susannah ride? Where is he taking them?

2. What is ka-tet?

3. What is the code word for the five nuclear submarines Eddie finds?

4. Who feeds Roland and his companions at The Church of the Blood Everlasting?

5. What is graf?

6. What is the name of Jake's pet dog?

7. Who asks Jake to give him his watch?

8. What is the monorail's cruising speed?

9. According to the monorail computer, what is the difference between a cat and a complex sentence?

10. According to Roland, what is the difference between a grandmother and a granary?

11. What is Mr. Bissette's phone number?

12. What is the phone number for the sales office of Turtle Bay Luxury Condominiums?

13. What does it say on the sign painted in the window of Calvin Tower's bookstore?

14. What are the first four lines of Jack's school essay, "My Understanding of the Truth"?

15. What large creature looks like a badger crossed with a raccoon, and has a long, furcovered tail?

16. What large kingdom once dominated the earth in early times?

17. Where is The Mansion located?

18. What kind of canned food does Jake find next to the dead rat in the kitchen cabinet?

19. Who threatens Roland with a grenade?

20. What type of pen do the businessmen Jake meets play tick-tack-toe with?

THE DARK HALF

1. What is Thad Beaumont's pen name?

2. Who is the sheriff of Castle Rock, Maine?

3. Which of Thad Beaumont's novels was nominated for the National Book Award in 1972?
   (a) *Air Dance*
   (b) *Dancing Under Water*
   (c) *The Sudden Dance*
   (d) *Dark Dances*
   (e) *Dancing With the Devil*

4. What issue of *People* magazine runs a feature article on Thad Beaumont?

5. What is the inscription on George Stark's tombstone?

6. What are the names of Thad's twin children?

7. Who is the main character of the novel *Machine's Way?*

8. What type of truck does George Stark drive? What type of car did he drive in Thad's dreams?

9. Who is in charge of the Castle Rock Public Works Department?

10. What kind of bird is capable of destroying George Stark?

11. What is the number on the license plate of Homer Gamache's 1971 Chevrolet pickup truck?

12. What brand of pen does Thad write with? What brand of pencil?

13. Where does George Stark keep his .32 caliber pistol?

14. What course does Thad Beaumont teach at the University of Maine?

15. What is the title of Thad Beaumont's first short story, published when he was eleven?

16. Who performs brain surgery on Thad Beaumont? What does he find in Thad's cranium during the surgery?

17. What does Machine do to Halstead?

18. What type of ammunition does Stark use in his .45 revolver?

19. Who teaches the Folk Myth seminar at the University of Maine?

20. What is the name of the novel Thad writes for George Stark?

NEEDFUL THINGS

1. Who is the proprietor of Needful Things?

2. Who runs the shop You Sew and Sew? What medical condition does she suffer from?

3. Which baseball card does Brian Rusk get at Needful Things?
   (a) Babe Ruth
   (b) Hank Aaron
   (c) Tom Seaver
   (d) Sandy Koufax
   (e) Lou Gehrig

4. What is the name of the church in Castle Rock, Maine? The town tavern?

5. How much money does the judge in small claims court order Eddie Warburton to pay Sonny Jackett?
   (a) $50
   (b) $150
   (c) $250

(d) $350
(e) $500

6. What item at Needful Things does Cora Rusk want to buy?

7. What firm installed the track lighting in Needful Things?

8. What does Cyndi Rose buy from Needful Things?

9. Where did Mr. Gaunt live before he moved to Castle Rock?

10. What is the name of Castle Rock's Head Selectman?

11. Which of the following does Hugh Priest trade at Needful Things for a fox tail?
(a) a baseball card
(b) $1.50 in change
(c) a roll of Certs
(d) a crisp new $100 bill
(e) his soul

12. How tall is Norris Ridgewick? What nickname do the other deputies in the Castle Rock police department give him?

13. What item in the window of Needful Things attracts Norris's interest?

14. What phone number does the bumper sticker on Wilma Jerzyck's car tell you to call if you don't like her driving?

15. How much does Sally Ratcliffe pay at Needful Things for a splinter of petrified wood from the Holy Land?

16. Who is the head custodian at the Municipal Building?

17. What is the name of Alan Pangborn Jr.'s college room-mate?

18. What brand of cordless phone did Mr. Gaunt own?

19. What type of Egyptian amulet does Gaunt give Polly to ward off arthritis pain?

20. Who becomes Leland Gaunt's driver?

GERALD'S GAME

1. What is Gerald's profession?
   (a) doctor
   (b) dentist
   (c) accountant
   (d) lawyer
   (e) engineer

2. On what day does Jessie witness a total eclipse of the sun?

3. On what lake is Gerald and Jessie's summer home?

4. How old is Gerald Burlingame when he dies of a heart attack?
   (a) 30
   (b) 35
   (c) 40
   (d) 45
   (e) 50
   (f) 55

5. Who is "Mr. Happy"?

6. Who was the original owner of Prince?

7. Where is Sunset Trails located?

8. Who is the escaped lunatic who terrorizes Jesse when she is handcuffed to the bed in her cabin?

9. What is Exhibit 217?

10. What type of handcuffs does Gerald own?

11. Who sexually abuses Jessie when she is a child?

12. Who is the local TV sportscaster?

13. Who did Jessie think of as a "boring old blue-haired booger"?

14. What is the name of the female voice Jesse hears in her head?

15. What is the ninth-biggest lake in Maine?

16. Who was Jessie's therapist?

17. Ruth Neary sends Jessie a postcard showing a picture of a man with his tongue sticking out. What is the caption on the picture?

18. Where does Castle County Sheriff Norris Ridgewick find Joubert laying in an open coffin with an ax in his hand?

19. With whom does Jessie stay after she is rescued?

20. What color trenchcoat does Doug Rowe wear on TV?

DOLORES CLAIBORNE

1. What does Dolores Claiborne's daughter do for a living?
   (a) runway model
   (b) call girl
   (c) corporate executive
   (d) writer
   (e) home maker

2. Where does Dolores Claiborne live?

3. What are the names of the police officers that question Dolores Claiborne?

4. Who did Dolores Claiborne murder?

5. How many acres does Dolores Claiborne own?
   (a) one
   (b) three
   (c) six
   (d) ten
   (e) sixty

6. How did Vera Donovan's husband die?

7. What is Hattie McLeod's name for social security?

8. Who was Vera Donovan's doctor?

9. With what cleanser did Vera Donovan insist her tubs be scrubbed with?
   (a) Lestoil
   (b) Top Job
   (c) Mr. Clean
   (d) Spic and Span
   (e) Pine Sol

10. What child does Joe St. George sexually abuse?

11. How does Joe St. George die? Where is he buried?

12. What is the name of the medical examiner who suspects foul play in Joe's death? Where is he from?

13. How much does Norris Pinette pay Dolores Claiborne for Joe's shortwave radio?
    (a) $10
    (b) $15
    (c) $25
    (d) $35
    (e) $50

14. How old is Dolores?
    (a) 45
    (b) 55
    (c) 60
    (d) 65
    (e) 67

15. What type of household mess is Vera Donovan obsessed with?

16. How does Vera die?

17. What is the name of the mailman on Tall Island?

18. Who becomes the City Manager in Machias?

19. What brand of fine china does Vera Donovan own?

20. How much money does Dolores Claiborne inherit from Vera Donovan?
    (a) $1 million
    (b) $10 million
    (c) $500,000
    (d) $20 million
    (e) $30 million

INSOMNIA

1. What was the cover price on the first hardcover edition of *Insomnia?* How many pages was the book?

2. At what supermarket does Ralph Roberts buy his groceries?

3. What does Carolyn Roberts die from? Who is her physician?

4. Who are the Harrison Avenue Crocks?

5. Which of Ralph's neighbors exhibits paranoid and psychotic behavior resulting in violence?

6. What political activist is coming to speak at a rally in Derry, Maine? Which of the books she authored won the Pulitzer Prize? What is the topic of the book?

7. What is the name of the abortion clinic in Derry?

THE ULTIMATE UNAUTHORIZED STEPHEN KING TRIVIA CHALLENGE

8. Which of the following newspapers does Ralph Roberts read daily?
   (a) *The Maine Herald*
   (b) *USA Today*
   (c) *The Derry Daily Press*
   (d) *The Boston Globe*
   (e) *The New York Times*

9. What is the prolife activist group in Derry?

10. What is the name of the used book store on the corner of Witcham and Main?

11. What is the name of Doc #1? Doc #2?

12. Who is an agent of the Random?

13. What does the bumper sticker read on the back of Helen Deepneau's reconditioned Volvo?

14. What does Helen wear on her blouses to symbolize that she has become a lesbian?

15. What is the name of the Red King?

16. Whom does Ralph Roberts marry after his wife Carolyn passes away? Who is the maid of honor at the wedding?

17. With what firm did Ed Deepneau have a life insurance policy?

18. When Ralph thinks he has colon cancer in the fall of 1996, what does it turn out to be?

19. What does Atropos call Ralph? What does Ralph call Atropos?

20. Whose life does Ralph save when he is hit by a car and killed?

ROSE MADDER

1. What does Norman do for a living?
   (a) FBI agent
   (b) mobster
   (c) police officer
   (d) security guard
   (e) gym owner

2. What prompts Rose McClendon Daniels to finally leave her husband?

3. What words are stamped on Norman's ring?

4. What kind of chair is Pooh's Chair?

5. Where does Rose trade her wedding ring for a $75 painting?

6. Who offers Rose a job recording audio books?

7. Who is Norman Daniels's favorite movie actor?

(a) Clint Eastwood
(b) James Coburn
(c) Charles Bronson
(d) George Peppard
(e) Arnold Schwarzenegger

8. What supernatural being does Rose meet when she enters the oil painting?

9. With whom does Rose fall in love after she leaves Norman?

10. What is the address of Rose's new apartment?

11. What is the name of Bill and Rose's daughter? How much does she weigh at birth?

12. What is the address of the Daughters and Sisters shelter for battered women?

13. For what organization does Peter Slowik do volunteer work?

14. What disgusting thing does Gert Kinshaw do to Norman when they fight?

15. What color is Cynthia's punk hairdo?

16. What coffee shop do Rose and Pam frequent?

17. What insects come out of Rose's painting?

18. What odd nervous habit does Norman Daniels have?

19. Where is the ninth annual Daughters and Sisters "Swing into Summer" picnic and concert held?

20. Who was Norman's favorite porn star?

THE GREEN MILE

1. How tall is John Coffey? How much does he weigh?

2. What nickname do the prison guards give the electric chair?

3. What is the name of Eduard Delacroix's pet mouse?

4. Where did Paul Edgecombe work as a prison guard? What nursing home did he end up in?

5. Who calls Alzheimer's "AIDS for old people"?

6. In what year was John Coffey wrongly convicted and jailed for the murder of the Detterick Twins?
   (a) 1930
   (b) 1931
   (c) 1932
   (d) 1933
   (e) 1934

7. Who is the meanest and cruelest prison guard on the E Block? Who is the biggest?

8. Who does John Coffey cure of cancer through his healing power?

9. How many installations are there in *The Green Mile* serial thriller?

10. With whom does Paul Edgecombe fall in love after his retirement?

11. What comes out of John Coffey's mouth after he heals someone of a major illness?

12. What does Melinda Moores give John Coffey as a gift for saving her life?

13. From what college does Paul Edgecombe's granddaughter, Tessa, graduate?

14. How old is Paul Edgecombe's pet mouse when it dies? How old is Paul Edgecombe at the time?

15. What is William Wharton's nickname?

16. What does John Coffey request for his last meal?
    (a) steak
    (b) ribs
    (c) turkey
    (d) meatloaf
    (e) bacon and eggs

17. Where was Eva Price's boarding house located?

18. Who shoots William Wharton to death in his cell?

19. Where do people in the nursing home where Paul Edgecombe lives go to watch TV?

20. What is the name of the local reporter who covered John Coffey's trial?

DESPERATION

1. What essay written by Johnny Marinville generated the fourth-largest volume of letters ever sent to *Life* magazine in response to one of their stories?

2. What does Mary Jackson see nailed to a speed-limit sign on U.S. 50?

3. What was the name and location of the biggest open-pit copper mine in the 1960s and '70s?

4. When gambling, what is the maximum amount Ralph Carver will allow himself to lose before he quits?
   (a) $500
   (b) $1000
   (c) $2000
   (d) $5000
   (e) $10,000

5. What rock group did Steve Ames tour with for eight months?
   (a) Kiss

(b) Black Sabbath
(c) Genesis
(d) The Rolling Stones
(e) Devo

6. What is the name of the evil entity that possesses the police officer in Desperation, Nevada?

7. What is the name of the police chief in Desperation? His two deputies?

8. What company ran the copper mines in Desperation?

9. Which of the following taverns are located in or near Desperation, Nevada?
(a) Bud's Suds
(b) Pink's Drinks
(c) Lift the Latch
(d) The Owl and I
(e) The Broken Drum

10. Who escapes from Tak's prison first?
(a) Collie Entragian
(b) Steve Ames
(c) David Carver
(d) Johnny Marinville
(e) Frank Dodd

11. What is the name of Tak's place, the well of the worlds?

12. How many people are trapped in the China Shaft when the mine caves in in 1959?
(a) 12
(b) 21
(c) 35
(d) 51

(e) 61

(f) 211

13. What was John Marinville's wallet made of? How much money was in it?

14. What is David Carver's home address?

15. What is the title of the book of essays Terry wants Johnny Marinville to write?

16. What is the name of the casino in Desperation, Nevada? What does the sign in its window say?

17. After soma dies and pneuma departs, what remains?

18. What is a waisin?

19. What physically happens to people when they are possessed by the demon from the mine?

20. What nickname does Tak give David Carver?

PART TWO

THE BACHMAN BOOKS

RAGE

1. What was the original title of *Rage*?

2. Who commented that *Rage* is "full of windy psychological preachments"?

3. What high school does Joe McKennedy attend?

4. Who takes Sandra Cross to the Wonderland dance?

5. Where does Pete McKennedy work?

6. In which prison was Flapper Keene serving time?

7. Who goes crazy and holds his high school class hostage with a rifle? Of whose murders is he convicted?

8. What is the title of Carol Granger's valedictory speech? In what national magazine was it reprinted?

9. Who does Ted Jones cheat off of in French class?

10. What does Al Lathrop do for a living?

11. What is the combination to Charlie Decker's high school locker?

12. Whose father was vice president of the Pacerville Bank and Trust?

13. Who became the chief of police after Warren Talbot passed away in 1975?

14. Who swallows a mouse raw?

15. What kind of car does Dicky Cable have?

16. Who shoots Charlie Decker after Charlie lets his hostages go?

17. Which of the high school hostages becomes permanently catatonic?

18. Who sentences Charlie to be remanded to the Augusta State Hospital and treated for insanity?

19. According to Charlie, where is it "a treat to beat your meat"?

20. What is a "Cherokee Nose Job"?

THE LONG WALK

1. At the start of the Long Walk, how much does Peter McVries weigh? How much does Ray Garraty weigh?

2. What number walker is Arthur Baker in the Long Walk? What number is Garraty? McVries?

3. Who is the commander of the Army?

4. How fast do you have to walk to avoid getting a warning? How many consecutive warnings disqualify a walker?

5. What is "Hint 13"?

6. What is the longest distance a Walk has gone without any of the Walkers dropping out?

7. What is "Hint 6"?

8. Which of the Walkers is shot because he gets a cramp

in his leg and can't keep up with the minimum speed requirement?

9. What is "Hint 3"?

10. What brand of cracker does Garraty have for supper with cheese and tuna fish?

11. What is "Rule 8"?

12. What words are imprinted on Fenter's T-shirt?

13. What Walker does the Aroostook County Parents' Association root for?
    (a) Barker
    (b) Garraty
    (c) Barkovitch
    (d) Rodman
    (e) Anelli

14. What Walker is shot when he becomes unconscious from sunstroke?

15. Who gives free watermelon to the Walkers?

16. How many participants each year have their name drawn for the Long Walk, to be Walkers or backups?
    (a) 50
    (b) 100
    (c) 150
    (d) 200
    (e) 250

17. What essay do potential Walkers have to write as part of the entrance exam for getting into the Long Walk?

18. What month of the year is "Confirm Your Sex Month"?

19. Which Walker loses his mind during the Long Walk?

20. Which Walker is the Major's son?

ROADWORK

1. What subtitle appears on the front cover of the original edition of *Roadwork?*

2. Where does Barton George Dawes buy his weapons?

3. Who does Dawes call from the gun shop?

4. What is Dawes's home address? What kind of house does he live in?

5. What is Harold Swinnerton's business phone number?

6. For what book does Dawes get an overdue notice from the library?

7. What corporation purchased the Blue Ribbon Laundry?

8. What brand of cigarette does Vinnie Mason smoke?

9. The construction of what roadway forces Bart Dawes and his wife to move out of their house?

10. How much did Ray Tarkington loan Bart Dawes to go back to college and get a degree? What was the interest rate on the loan?

11. Which of the following businesses are clients of the Blue Ribbon Laundry?
(a) McDonald's
(b) Howard Johnson
(c) Central Hospital
(d) Quality Motor Court
(e) Vinnie's Go-Go

12. Who is Bart's boss? What kind of car does he drive?

13. What is the estimated cost to renovate the new Waterford laundry and dry cleaning plant?
(a) $100,000
(b) $250,000
(c) $50,000
(d) $1 million
(e) $75,000

14. How did Bart's son, Charles, die?

15. In what prison did Magliore do an 18-month stretch for receiving stolen property?

16. What is Bart Dawes's "private drink"?

17. What is the lunch special at Handy Andy's?

18. Which of the following cars does Bart Dawes's father-in-law own?
(a) Lincoln Towncar
(b) Cadillac Gran DeVille
(c) Bonneville station wagon

(d) Volkswagen Bug
(e) Mercedes Benz

19. Which of the following dolls does Bart Dawes buy as Christmas gifts for his nieces?
(a) Raggedy Ann
(b) Maisie the Acrobat
(c) Chatty Cathy
(d) Baby Wet-Myself
(e) Sleepy Sally

20. When the Blue Ribbon Laundry closes, where does Tom Granger get a job?

THE RUNNING MAN

1. Who played Ben Richards in the film version of *The Running Man*?

2. Where do Ben Richards and his family live?

3. On what TV game show do sick people run a treadmill to win prize money?

4. The billboard across the street from Ben's apartment building has a thermometer. What product does it advertise? What is the product slogan?

5. How old is Ben Richards? How tall? How much does he weigh? What is his IQ? What size uniform does he wear?

6. What is Richards served for breakfast after his first night at the Games Building
   (a) cold cereal
   (b) waffles
   (c) French toast

(d) scrambled eggs
(e) fresh-squeezed orange juice

7. Who administers the written Game test to Ben?

8. Match the words in the word association test given to Ben Richards—from the words given, in the left column, to Richards's answers, in the right.

(1)	Doctor	(a)	Murder
(2)	Penis	(b)	Out
(3)	Red	(c)	Dagger
(4)	Silver	(d)	Tests
(5)	Rifle	(e)	Black
(6)	Win	(f)	Money
(7)	Sex	(g)	Cock
(8)	Strike	(h)	Nigger

9. What is Arthur M. Burns's official title?

10. From what part-time job was Jimmy Laughlin fired for taking part in a sit-down strike?

11. What law makes racial prejudice illegal?

12. Which of the following does Richards identify during an inkblot test?
(a) bats
(b) two women killing
(c) a sports car
(d) a sick person
(e) excrement

13. Who is the executive producer of *The Running Man?*

14. Who is the head Hunter? For how long must Richards

evade the Hunters to win the Grand Prize? What is the Grand Prize?

15. What does Richards order for dinner after he is chosen as a contestant?

16. What are the titles of the three books the Games Bell-boy brings Richards to read in his suite?

17. Who is the host of *The Running Man?* The director?

18. How much does a *Running Man* contestant get paid for killing a Hunter?
    (a) $10,000
    (b) $50,000
    (c) $100,000
    (d) $150,000
    (e) nothing

19. What kind of airplane does Richards fly into the Games Building to kill Arthur Killian?

20. What kind of coffeemaker did Sheila, Ben's wife, always want?

THINNER

1. What is the name of Conley's company?

2. What bridge do the gypsies take when they leave Bangor?

3. Who does Billy Halleck hit and kill with his car?

4. What does Taduz's curse, "thinner," do to Billy?

5. What type of pie does Taduz Lemke give to Billy?

6. Who owns the Three Brothers Restaurant?

7. What is Leon Enders's nickname?

8. Who was found with a bullet hole in his head and a chicken cut open in his lap?

9. The decal of what college is affixed to the back window of the Porsche driven by the five rich kids?

10. To what New Jersey clinic is Billy Hallek sent for metabolic tests?

11. What is "The House That Budweiser Built"?

12. What inside of Billy causes him to grow thinner?

13. What textbook is Gina Lemke reading when Ginelli questions her?

14. What were the ingredients of the substance with which Ginelli poisons Taduz Lemke's pit bulls?

15. What judge finds Billy Halleck not at fault in the vehicular manslaughter of the old gypsy woman?

16. What type of weapon does Ginelli receive wrapped in a package marked "World Book Encyclopedia"?

17. Where is the Frenchman's Bay Motel located?

18. Where does the Halleck family live?

19. What type of car does Mrs. Houston drive?

20. How much money did the Rossington family pay for a reproduction of an 1880s New York streetlamp from the Horschow collection?

THE REGULATORS

1. Where does Katherine Anne Goodlowe live?

2. What is the name of Audrey Wyler's 8-year-old autistic nephew?

3. According to Charles Verrill, what year did Richard Bachman pass away? Who found the manuscript of *The Regulators* in a box in Bachman's cellar?

4. Where is the E-Z Stop 24 located? Who is the new clerk?

5. Whose house is on the northeast corner of Bear Street and Poplar Street?

6. What type of business does Mary Jackson work for?

7. What is the name of the newspaper delivery boy who delivers *The Shopper* to the residents of Poplar Street in Wentworth, Ohio, on Monday afternoons?

8. What moving company had a warehouse on Anderson Avenue?

9. What is the title of the book John Marinville wrote about a man having a love affair with his daughter?
   (a) *Gerald's Game*
   (b) *Total Eclipse*
   (c) *Delight*
   (d) *The Affair*
   (e) *Rage of Angels*

10. What is Seth's favorite TV show?

11. What is the name of the main character in the children's books John Marinville wrote?

12. What is the name of the Reeds' dog? What type of dog is he?

13. What is Steve Ames's motto in life?

14. In what key does John Marinville want to strum his guitar and sing *The Ballad of Jesse James*?
   (a) A
   (b) B flat
   (c) C
   (d) D
   (e) E sharp

15. Who is the concierge at Mohonk Mountain House?

16. What kind of car did Mary Jackson drive?
   (a) Taurus
   (b) Lumina
   (c) Accord

(d) Camry

(e) Eldorado

17. What is the title of episode 55 of *Motokops?* Who wrote it?

18. What was Steve Ames's original major at MIT?

19. Which of the following actors appear in the TV movie, *The Regulators?*
    (a) John Payne
    (b) John Wayne
    (c) Ty Hardin
    (d) Karen Steele
    (e) Rory Calhoun

20. What kills Gary Soderson by tearing his throat out with its teeth?

PART THREE

THE SHORT STORIES

NIGHT SHIFT

1. In "Suffer the Little Children" why does the teacher lure her students into the mimeograph room and murder them, one by one?

2. What short story from *Night Shift* was later expanded by King into the novel *'Salem's Lot*?

3. What short story from this collection was later expanded by King into the novel *The Stand*?

4. What is the name of the high school English teacher in "Sometimes They Come Back"?

5. How much money did Hall get paid working as a picker-machine operator at the mill in Gates Falls, Maine?

6. What is the medical nomenclature for the super-flu called Captain Tripps?

7. What is the DESA?

8. What make and model laundry machine is the mangler?

9. What is Lester Billings afraid of?

10. Richie Grenadine is mutated by drinking a spoiled case of what brand of beer?

11. What is the minimum fee hit man Johnny Renshaw charges to kill someone?
    (a) $1000
    (b) $5000
    (c) $10,000
    (d) $50,000
    (e) $100,000

12. What company makes the G.I. Joe Vietnam Footlocker toy?

13. Where does Jim Norman get a teaching job? What was his college grade point average?

14. What course does Chip Osway get an "F" in?

15. On what date did Strawberry Spring come to New Sharon Teachers' College?

16. With whom does Norris have an affair?

17. What is the phone number of the lawn service Harold Parkette hires to cut his grass?

18. What is the address of Quitters Inc.?

19. At what elementary school did Edward Jackson Hamner Jr. first see and fall in love with Elizabeth?

20. What is the population of Gatlin, Nebraska?

DIFFERENT SEASONS

1. What story from *Different Seasons* did Rob Reiner make into a motion picture?

2. What is the address of the Manhattan club David Adley visits?

3. What law firm does David Adley work for?

4. What words are inscribed above the fireplace at the club?

5. Who is the author of "These Were Our Brothers"?

6. What night is the best night for stories at the club?

7. What almost supernatural act does Sandra Stansfield perform?

8. Who is the author of *A Practical Guide to Pregnancy and Delivery*?

9. How old was Andy Dufresne when he was imprisoned

in Shawshank in 1948? Who was he found guilty of murdering?

10. Who was the golf pro at Falmouth Hills?

11. Which of the following types of rocks does Andy Dufresne collect and polish from the Shawshank prison yard?
(a) quartz
(b) mica
(c) shale
(d) limestone
(e) granite

12. How much money does Andy bring into prison hidden in one of his body cavities?

13. What kind of weapon does Bogs Diamond carry? What is engraved on its handle?

14. How much money does Byron Hadley inherit from his brother?

15. What newspaper is Todd Bowden a delivery boy for?

16. What is Arthur Denker's address? His real name?

17. What does Vern Tessio bury under his front porch?

18. What magazine publishes Gordon Lachance's story, "Stud City"?

19. What does Lard Ass Hogan get sick of eating?

20. How much cash does Andy leave for Red to find under a stone in a hay field?

35

SKELETON CREW

1. On what lake does the Mist first appear?

2. Who are the three third-grade teachers at the Acorn Street Grammar School?

3. Who hired Hal Shelburn after he was laid off from National Aerodyne?
   (a) The Shop
   (b) Project Arrow Head
   (c) IBM
   (d) Microsoft
   (e) Texas Instruments

4. What kind of gun did Curt Garrish's father give him for Christmas?

5. What year did Ophelia Todd disappear from Castle Rock, Maine?
   (a) 1971
   (b) 1972
   (c) 1973

(d) 1974
(e) 1975

6. Who invented the jaunt? When?

7. What is the name of Mike Scollay's overweight sister?

8. On what lake is the Raft located?

9. How much extra income does Richard Hagstrom earn each year by moonlighting as a writer?
   (a) $1000
   (b) $2500
   (c) $5000
   (d) $10,000
   (e) $20,000

10. Who kills himself by shaking his own hand?

11. What is the serial number of the spaceship Shapiro and Rand crash in?

12. For how much money is the Delver looking glass in Samuel Claggert's insured?

13. What is the name of Ace Merrill's girlfriend?

14. What does surgeon Richard Pine do to survive when he is stranded on an island?

15. What model truck does Uncle Otto have?

16. For what company does the Milkman make morning deliveries?

17. What is Dr. Arlinder's phone number?

18. Who is the author of *Underworld Figures?*

19. Where does Stella Flanders live?

20. Who built the Word Processor of the Gods?

36

FOUR PAST MIDNIGHT

1. At what gate does American Pride flight L1011 arrive and deplane?
   (a) 11
   (b) 22
   (c) 33
   (d) 44
   (e) 2A

2. What is "Teasing the Geese"?

3. What supernatural creatures are responsible for helping time move forward by obliterating the past?

4. What kind of camera does Kevin Delevan get for his birthday?

5. Who runs the Emporium Galorium?

6. Who is the Library Policeman?

7. What flight travels back in time?

8. What disability does Dinah Bellman have?

9. What is Albert Kaussner's nickname?

10. Who is "Her Majesty's Mechanic"?

11. How many mystery novels has Robert Jenkins written?

12. With whom does Craig Toomey have a 9 A.M. meeting in Boston?

13. Where does Nick Hopewell's father live?

14. On what lake is Mort Rainey's house in Maine? What was the title of his first best-seller?

15. Where does John Shooter live?

16. With what real estate agent does Amy Rainey have an affair?

17. What does Chaffee put on his Spam sandwiches?

18. What does Kevin Delevan get for his sixteenth birthday?

19. At what time did The Event that sent Brian Engle's flight back in time take place?

20. What did Dave Duncan do for a living?

NIGHTMARES & DREAMSCAPES

1. What kind of Cadillac does James Dolan own?

2. How is Elizabeth Robinson killed?

3. What is Dolan's address?

4. What is Howard Fornoy's nickname?

5. What town has no crime because of a chemical in the water supply?

6. How much money does Briggs Sheridan owe Mr. Reggie?
   (a) $7000
   (b) $17,000
   (c) $27,000
   (d) $70,000
   (e) $71,500.25

7. What kind of creature is Popsy?

8. What newspaper is Richard Dees a reporter for?

9. Gloria Swett weighs 200 pounds. What is her nickname?

10. What does George Banning say is a "pretty pony"?

11. How was George's son, Billy Banning, killed?

12. What happens in the town of Willow, Maine every seven years?

13. What subject were John and Elise Graham researching on their summer sabbatical?

14. What does Howard Mitla see crawling around in his bathroom sink?
    (a) a cockroach
    (b) a scorpion
    (c) a living eyeball
    (d) a dismembered human finger
    (e) a three-inch-tall naked woman

15. What is the name of the Russian cosmonaut on the Gorbachev/Truman spacecraft?

16. What flavor ice cream did Patty Vanchockstraw always order at the Dave's Drugs ice cream counter?
    (a) vanilla
    (b) strawberry
    (c) chocolate mint chip
    (d) rainbow
    (e) chocolate

17. Which of the following novels did Peter Jeffries write?
    (a) *The Sons of Summer*

(b) *Boys in the Mist*
(c) *Gorillas in the Hood*
(d) *Blaze of Glory*
(e) *Heaven and Earth*

18. At what hotel is Martha Rosewall a maid?

19. Where do John Tell and Paul Janning mix the latest album of the heavy metal group, The Dead Beats? What is the name of the album?

20. What is the name of Lord and Lady Hulls's middle son?

PART FOUR

MOVIES AND TV

STEPHEN KING
AT THE MOVIES

1. Which of the following actors did *not* appear in the movie *Carrie?*
   (a) John Travolta
   (b) Amy Irving
   (c) Piper Laurie
   (d) William Katz
   (e) Ron Howard

2. Who directed *The Shining?*

3. Who played Jordy Verrill in the movie *Creepshow?*

4. Who directed *Christine?*
   (a) George Romero
   (b) Stanley Kubrick
   (c) John Carpenter
   (d) Wes Craven
   (e) Gary Rubin

5. What *E.T.* actress played Tad's mother in *Cujo?*

6. Who played Greg Stillson in *The Dead Zone*?

7. What former *thirtysomething* actor starred in *Children of the Corn*?

8. What did *Carrie* cost to make? How much did it gross at the box office?

9. Who starred as Carrie White in the Broadway musical version?

10. Who plays the vampire Barlow in the TV movie *'Salem's Lot*? Who plays Straker?

11. Who plays Hallorann in the movie version of *The Shining*?

12. Which of the following stories is *not* part of the film *Creepshow*?
    (a) "Sometimes They Come Back"
    (b) "Father's Day"
    (c) "The Crate"
    (d) "They're Creeping Up on You"
    (e) "The Ring"

13. What former Cheers star plays Harry Wentworth in *Creepshow*?
    (a) George Wendt
    (b) Woody Harrelson
    (c) John Ratzenberger
    (d) Ted Danson
    (e) Harry Anderson

14. How many cockroaches were used in the filming of *Creepshow*?

15. How many different Saint Bernards played *Cujo* in the movie?

16. Who directed *The Dead Zone*? What is the subtitle of the movie?

17. How many 1958 Plymouth Furies were used in the filming of *Christine*?

18. What two short films are on the video titled *Stephen King's Night Shift Collection*?

19. Who directed *Firestarter*?

20. What three stories comprise the film *Cat's Eye*?

21. In what Stephen King film does Gary Busey have a major role?

22. Who directed *Maximum Overdrive*?

23. In what Stephen King movie does Richard Dreyfuss play a writer?

24. In what Stephen King movie does Daryl Hannah's younger sister Paige appear?

25. Who plays TV game show host Damon Killian in *The Running Man*?

26. What former *Munsters* star plays Dr. Louis Creed's next-door neighbor in *Pet Sematary*?

27. Which segment of the *Tales From the Darkside* movie is based on a Stephen King short story?
(a) "Lover's Vow"

(b) "Cat From Hell"
(c) "Lot 249"
(d) "Jerusalem's Lot"
(e) "Prayers for the Dead"

28. In what Stephen King film does Brad Dourif play an exterminator?

29. Aside from *Stand by Me,* what other Stephen King film did Rob Reiner direct?

30. What is the title of the original screenplay Stephen King wrote for Michael Jackson?

39

KING TV

1. What was the running time of *'Salem's Lot* when it was originally broadcast as a TV miniseries? How much was cut from it when it was shown as a TV movie?

2. On what syndicated TV series was "The Word Processor of the Gods" broadcast as an episode in 1986?

3. Who wrote the teleplay of the Stephen King short story "Gramma" for its adaptation as a *Twilight Zone* episode?

4. What is the name of the horror novelist in "Sorry, Right Number," an original screenplay written by Stephen King for George Romero's TV series?

5. In what Stephen King TV adaptation does Pierce Brosnan appear?

6. In what Stephen King TV movie does John Ritter star?

7. What former *Night Court* actor appeared in the three-part television special, *Stephen King's World of Horror?*

8. In what Stephen King TV movie does Tim Matheson star as a young teacher who had a nervous breakdown?

9. What happens to the janitor played by Keith Szarabajka in Stephen King's *Golden Years?*

10. In what Stephen King TV movie does *NYPD Blue* star Jimmy Smits have a major role?

11. What *Forrest Gump* star appears in the TV version of *The Stand?*

12. In what Stephen King TV movie does basketball player Kareem Abdul-Jabbar appear?

13. What *Wings* star played Jack Torrance in the TV miniseries of *The Shining?*

14. What *Rocky Horror Picture Show* actor plays the evil clown in the TV miniseries *It?*

15. What happens to Harlam Williams whenever his eyes glow green?

16. In what TV movie did Stephen King play a bus driver?

17. What drug is Dr. Ackerman addicted to?

18. Who played Wendy Torrance in Stephen King's TV remake of *The Shining?*

PART FIVE

STEPHEN KING, UP CLOSE AND PERSONAL

PROFESSIONAL
LIFE

1. What type of word processor does King use? How many words does he write each day?

2. What was the last Stephen King novel to feature the fictional town of Castle Rock, Maine?

3. What are the two Stephen King novels set in Colorado?

4. In what monster movie was the main character a young boy wearing a red "Stephen King Rules" T-shirt?

5. According to Stephen King, an aspiring horror writer should give up after receiving how many rejection slips from publishers and editors?

6. Which of his novels did Stephen King delay publication of because he thought it was too frightening?

7. What does Stephen King refer to as "eyeglasses for the mind"?

8. Who calls Stephen King's work "plain fiction for plain folk"?

9. Which three Stephen King books were reviewed together in one article in the October 20, 1996 edition of the *New York Times Book Review*?

10. Approximately how many pages of fiction has Stephen King published in his career?

11. Which Stephen King film, critically well received and a financial success, did Stephen King say he found too arty?

12. What novelist interviewed Stephen King for *Playboy*?

13. How much did a signed first edition of Stephen King's 1981 nonfiction book *Danse Macabre* sell for at auction in New York, in October 1993?
   (a) $87
   (b) $870
   (c) $1870
   (d) $18,700
   (e) $187,000

14. To promote which of his novels did Stephen King tour the U.S.A. on his Harley Davidson motorcycle?

15. What was the quantity of the first printing of the hardcover edition of *Rose Madder*?

16. According to Shirley Sonderegger, Stephen King's secretary, how many languages have his books been translated into?
   (a) 5
   (b) 10

(c) 15
(d) 20
(e) 30

17. How many books has Stephen King sold?

18. What did Stephen King get paid for the movie rights to *Carrie?*

19. In what magazine did Stephen King first get a short story published? What was he paid for it?

20. What is the title of the prologue Stephen King wrote that was left out of the published version of *The Shining?*

PERSONAL LIFE

1. How many rooms are in Stephen King's Victorian mansion?

2. What are the call letters of the Maine radio station King owns? What format is the station?

3. What do Stephen King, Christopher Reeve, Ed Begley Jr. and Craig T. Nelson have in common?

4. Before Stephen's father changed it to King, what was his last name?

5. Which of the following is Stephen King afraid of?
   (a) bugs
   (b) elevators
   (c) airplanes
   (d) the dark
   (e) raw oysters
   (f) rats

6. Whom does Stephen King refer to as "a dickey bird on the back of civilization"?

7. Name King's three children.

8. When he was a child, what did King's mother give him to combat his fear of the dark?

9. Where do Stephen King's sons go to college?

10. Where did Stephen King teach English in 1971? What was his salary?

11. What was the name of the column Stephen King wrote for the University of Maine's weekly newspaper?

12. Where did Stephen King attend high school? What year did he graduate?

13. What does Stephen King say is "the best of the low emotions"?
    (a) fear
    (b) horror
    (c) terror
    (d) revulsion
    (e) disdain

14. Which of the following does Stephen King rate as among his favorite horror movies of all time?
    (a) *The Texas Chainsaw Massacre*
    (b) *Night of the Living Dead*
    (c) *Freaks*
    (d) *Invasion of the Body Snatchers*
    (e) *Psycho*

15. Which of the following radio shows did Stephen King listen to when he was a child?
    (a) *The Inner Sanctum*
    (b) *The Swinging Door*
    (c) *I Love a Mystery*
    (d) *Dimension X*
    (e) *The Crawling Eye*

16. Where was Stephen King born?

17. What series of science fiction novels did Stephen King enjoy when he first began to read fiction?

18. What magazine called Stephen King "the dark Disney"? What publication called him "the Bard of Blood"?

19. To what magazines did Donald King, Stephen King's father, submit horror stories?

20. How much money did Stephen and Tabitha King announce in 1997 they were donating to the University of Maine?
    (a) $1 million
    (b) $2 million
    (c) $3 million
    (d) $4 million
    (e) $500,000

TABITHA KING

1. In what fictional Maine town are most of Tabitha King's novels set?

2. Which university awarded Tabitha King an honorary Ph.D.?

3. What does Tabitha King say she would do if Stephen King cheated on her?
   (a) give him one more chance
   (b) divorce him
   (c) shoot him
   (d) run him over with a 1958 Plymouth Fury
   (e) scare him so he has a fatal heart attack
   (f) put drugs in his food

4. How many brothers and sisters does Tabitha King have?
   (a) none
   (b) two
   (c) four
   (d) eight

(e) twelve

5. At what age did she complete her first novel?

6. What type of pet does Tabitha King have? What is his name?

7. What Tabitha King novel is about a woman who shrinks people?

8. In *Survivor,* what is Kissy Mellors's profession?

9. Where did Tabitha King and her husband first meet?

10. What is Tabitha King's official role with Maine Public Broadcasting?

A POTPOURRI OF KING TRIVIA

1. How many copies did *Carrie* sell in paperback?

2. To which of the following activities does Stephen King compare writing novels?
   (a) sex
   (b) drinking beer
   (c) riding a motorcycle
   (d) being a parent
   (e) swimming

3. To which of the following activities does Stephen King compare making a movie?
   (a) downhill skiing
   (b) football
   (c) baseball
   (d) ice skating
   (e) sex

4. What is the genetic makeup of the Sleepwalkers?

5. What real-life town gave Stephen King the inspiration for his book *Desperation?*

6. Who is Stephen King's foreign rights agent?

7. What gift was shrink-wrapped into 200,000 sets containing the two recent King novels *The Regulators* and *Desperation?* What promotional theme tied in with this gift?

8. What star from one of Stephen King's movies narrated the abridged audiotape version of *Desperation?*

9. What novelist and critic, in his review of Stephen King's novel *Rose Madder,* called the writing "ridiculous"?

10. How long is Rose McClendon married to Norman Daniels before she walks out on him?

11. What Stephen King character has muscles "popped like freshly risen bread rolls"?

12. What novelist once said of Stephen King, "He isn't capable of unplugging the word processor"?

13. For which of his books did Stephen King make a nationwide author's tour mostly to independent bookstores?

14. What novel did Stephen King call "the best suspense novel of the 1990s"? Who wrote it?

15. According to *New York* magazine (March 7, 1994), what is Stephen King's annual income?

16. What TV show did Stephen King tell *TV Guide* made him laugh hysterically?
    (a) *The New Cosby Show*
    (b) *Home Improvement*
    (c) *Grace Under Fire*
    (d) *Beavis and Butt-head*
    (e) *Family Matters*

17. What magazine called Stephen King "a one-man horror industry"?

18. Which of the following are removed from Thad Beaumont's skull when he has brain surgery as a youngster?
    (a) a blinking human eye
    (b) a talking pair of lips
    (c) teeth
    (d) a tongue
    (e) fingernails
    (f) hair
    (g) an ear

19. Who refers to Stephen King as "Bestsellasaurus Rex"?

20. Characters in various Stephen King novels and short stories have suffered which of the following grisly fates?
    (a) eaten by a giant maggot
    (b) decapitated by a werewolf
    (c) head ripped off and used as a bowling ball
    (d) a piece of piano wire stuck through the left eye into the brain
    (e) exploded after being overinflated with an air compressor
    (f) eaten by a giant mutant slug amoeba

21. Which of the following writers does Stephen King say he enjoys reading?
    (a) Elmore Leonard
    (b) Sara Paretsky
    (c) Robert Parker
    (d) Jonathan Kellerman
    (e) George Stark

22. Which of the following writers did Stephen King say he finds "unreadable"?
    (a) Joyce Carol Oates
    (b) James Michener
    (c) Robert Ludlum
    (d) John le Carré
    (e) Frederick Forsyth

23. According to Dolores Claiborne, what is sometimes an unhappy woman's best friend?

24. In *Rose Madder*, what is the name of the creature in the maze?
    (a) Minotaur
    (b) Erinyes
    (c) Atropos
    (d) Gorgon
    (e) Eclidilies

25. What amateur rock and roll band, comprised solely of authors, is Stephen King a guitarist for?

26. What film company was found in contempt of court for disobeying a court order to remove Stephen King's name from packaging and posters for videocassettes of *The Lawnmower Man*? How much money were they ordered to pay King?

27. What rating did the May 8, 1994 broadcast of *The Stand* receive?

28. Who directed *Shawshank Redemption?*

29. In what Stephen King short story does the son of a hotel maid win money from a slot machine?

30. Where was the TV version of *The Shining* filmed?

A POTPOURRI OF KING
TRIVIA, PART II

1. Which of the following towns did Stephen King live in or visit relatives in as a child?
   (a) Fort Wayne, Indiana
   (b) Stratford, Connecticut
   (c) Newark, New Jersey
   (d) Malden, Massachusetts
   (e) Powell, Maine

2. What was the original title of *'Salem's Lot*?
   (a) *The Homecoming*
   (b) *Second Coming*
   (c) *The Undead of Windham, Maine*
   (d) *The Night People*
   (e) *I Am Legion*

3. Which Stephen King book was nominated for a World Fantasy Award in 1976?

4. What is the first horror movie Stephen King remembers seeing?
   (a) *Dracula*

(b) *The Wolfman*
(c) *The Mummy*
(d) *Frankenstein*
(e) *Creature From the Black Lagoon*

5. What was the original title of *The Stand?*

6. In what George Romero horror movie, not based on a Stephen King story, does Stephen King have a cameo role?

7. What science fiction story of King's has been nominated for a Nebula Award?

8. What Stephen King book did *The Philadelphia Inquirer* call "one of the best books on American popular culture in the late 20th century"?

9. Which of Stephen King's relatives had "dowsing" ability and could find water with a piece of forked wood?

10. What is the name of the ghost said to haunt Stephen King's house?

11. Before he became a famous author, how much money did Stephen King earn pressing sheets in an industrial laundry?

12. Of what town does Stephen King say that, "If not the asshole of the universe, is at least within farting distance of it"?

13. What brand of vacuum cleaner did Stephen King's father sell?

14. Which of Stephen King's relatives liked to fry and then eat an entire loaf of bread in bacon droppings?

15. What did Stephen King tell *Playboy* magazine was his greatest fear?

16. What epitaph did Stephen King once say he wanted on his gravestone?

17. Which of the following jobs did Stephen King work at to support himself before he became financially successful as a writer?
    (a) bookkeeper
    (b) gas station attendant
    (c) repo man
    (d) bounty hunter
    (e) janitor

18. What varsity sport did King play in high school?
    (a) baseball
    (b) basketball
    (c) football
    (d) wrestling
    (e) tennis

19. In what amateur rock and roll band did Stephen King play rhythm guitar while a teenager?

20. Which of these leisure activities does Stephen King enjoy?
    (a) bowling
    (b) swimming
    (c) stamp collecting
    (d) beekeeping
    (e) poker

21. What type of writing does Stephen King say "feels too much like eating leftovers"?

22. What was the original title of "The Reach"?

23. Who published the original hardcover limited edition of *The Dark Tower?*

24. Who plays Danny Torrance in the ABC miniseries *The Shining?*

25. In what room in the Overlook is the naked lady ghost in the bathtub?
    (a) 177
    (b) 171
    (c) 217
    (d) 227
    (e) 272

26. What job does Audrey Wyler hold in Desperation, Nevada?

27 What is an adit?

28. What company owned The American West theater?

29. With what type of explosive does Johnny seal Tak in the mine?

30. What material was the special German edition of *Misery* bound in?

A STEPHEN KING MISCELLANY

1. For what financial services company did Stephen King appear in a TV commercial?

2. What is Stephen King's middle name?

3. What professional baseball team does Stephen King root for?

4. What unwritten Stephen King short story deals with rat infestation of an airline flight?

5. What religion is Stephen King?

6. How old was Stephen King when he began writing fiction?

7. Which writer does Stephen King say was his biggest influence?

8. What present did King buy his wife to celebrate the

paperback sale of *Carrie* to New American Library for a $400,000 advance? How much did it cost?

9. Which does Stephen King say is most important to him—his writing or his family?

10. For whom did Stephen King campaign in the 1984 presidential campaign?

11. What does Stephen King say is the most essential element of a good story?
(a) plot
(b) emotion
(c) characters
(d) tone
(e) setting
(f) mood

12. Through what publishing company did Stephen King self-publish *People, Places, Things* and *The Star Invaders?*

13. In which of the following towns did Stephen King *not* live when growing up?
(a) Scarborough, New York
(b) Croton-on-Hudson, New York
(c) Chicago, Illinois
(d) West De Pere, Wisconsin
(e) Fairbanks, Alaska

14. On what date did Stephen King and Tabitha Spruce get married?

15. What is the title of the comic book Stephen King co-authored?

16. In which of the following magazines has Stephen King published nonfiction articles?
    (a) *The New York Times Book Review*
    (b) *The Writer*
    (c) *Poets and Writers Newsletter*
    (d) *American Bookseller*
    (e) *The Journal of Horror Fiction*
    (f) *Rolling Stone College Papers*

17. In which of the following magazines has Stephen King published his poetry?
    (a) *Ankla*
    (b) *Onan*
    (c) *Ubris*
    (d) *Logos*
    (e) *Out of the Maine-Stream*

18. Which of the following is *not* a real title of a scholarly essay written about Stephen King?
    (a) "Apocalypse and the Popular Imagination"
    (b) "Cinderella's Revenge—Twists on Fairy-Tale and Mythic Themes in the Work of Stephen King"
    (c) "About Time—Temporal Propinquity in *The Langoliers*"
    (d) "Antidetection Gothic and Detective Conventions in the Fiction of Stephen King"
    (e) "The Destruction and Re-Creation of the Human Community in Stephen King's *The Stand*"

19. At what university have the Stephen King Archives been established?

20. Which of the following is *not* a working title of one of Stephen King's unpublished novels or short stories?
    (a) The Cannibals
    (b) Blaze

(c) The Aftermath
(d) Demonoid
(e) Welcome to Clearwater

21. Which of the following awards and honors has Stephen King won?
(a) Hugo Award
(b) World Fantasy Award
(c) O. Henry Award
(d) Bram Stoker Award
(e) Golden Pen Award

22. In what year was Stephen King a writer-in-residence at the University of Maine at Orono?

23. Which of the following books does Stephen King include on the list of his ten favorite fantasy horror novels of all time?
(a) *Dracula*
(b) *Frankenstein*
(c) *The Doll Who Ate His Mother*
(d) *Donovan's Brain*
(e) *The Crying of Lot 49*
(f) *The House on Haunted Hill*

24. What Stephen King book had the highest retail price? How much was it? What was unusual about its cover?

25. What was the name of the official Stephen King newsletter (now defunct)?

26. Which of Stephen King's books had a working digital clock built into the cover? Which was printed in a limited edition with a cover made of asbestos?

27. What is the title of Carlos Detweiler's unpublished horror novel?

28. What is the name of the publishing company Stephen King owns? What is the one book by an author other than King that it has published?

29. What race of aliens is Sun Corps a front for?

30. What unpublished Stephen King novel is about a large, mentally slow man who kidnaps a baby, planning to ransom it back to the child's rich parents, and then falls in love with the child instead?

31. What black activist lawyer sets off a race riot when he hits the town of Harding?

32. Who is the principal of Harding High School? With which of the students is he sexually obsessed?

33. What well-known New York theater critic gave a positive review of the musical *Carrie?*

34. Who owns the Shoeboat in the Derry Mall?

35. What character in *Firestarter* drinks three to four cokes a day?

36. What does Stephen King's brother David King do for a living?

37. According to Stephen King's Natal Astrological Chart, where was the moon at the time of his birth?

38. Of whom does Stephen King say, "He's the clumsiest, most awful writer. No style"?

39. Who called Stephen King's novels "The literary equivalent of a Big Mac and a large fries from McDonald's"?

40. How much money did ABC spend to make the 6-hour TV miniseries *The Shining?*
    (a) $3 million
    (b) $13 million
    (c) $23 million
    (d) $33 million
    (e) none—King financed the production out of his own pocket in exchange for which he keeps 90 percent of the advertising revenues

PART SIX

ANSWER KEY

ANSWERS

PART ONE: The Novels

1. CARRIE

1. Telekinesis—the ability to move objects with one's mind

2. Pig's blood

3. Nine months

4. Chamberlain, Maine

5. In the garbage

6. 70,000 words

7. Doubleday; $2500

8. New American Library; $400,000

9. *Getting It On, Babylon Here, Sword of the Darkness*

10. Bill Thompson

11. b, c

12. Crushed red velvet

13. 10:25

14. d

15. Billy Nolan; a 1961 Biscayne

16. Tommy Ross

17. A Webcor phonograph

18. Recited the prayer of exorcism from Deuteronomy

19. Chamberlain Mills & Weaving

20. Westover Doctor's Hospital

2. 'SALEM'S LOT

1. They turn into vampires

2. Eight months

3. Over 3 million

4. Romeo Poulin

5. New England Trucking Co.

6. Kurt Barlow; Richard Throckett Straker

7. 841–4000

8. b

9. c

10. $32,000

11. Bab's Beauty Boutique

12. *Air Dance*

13. $50

14. Burns Road, near the Harmony Hill graveyard

15. Continental Land Realty

16. Armour

17. Hubert Marsten

18. Carey Bryart

19. a, b, c

20. Father Callahan; Barlow makes him a vampire

3. THE SHINING

1. The Overlook Hotel

2. It is "murder" spelled backward

3. Over 4 million

4. It is turned into a writers' school

5. KMTX

6. c

7. Stuart Ullman

8. 6; 61

9. Stovington

10. d

11. May 5 to September 30

12. A Spanish llama .38

13. a, c

14. 300

15. Arthur Miller

16. Fun Time Automatic Machines

17. The "shining"

18. Vito the Chopper; indicted for an ax murder

19. b

4. THE STAND

1. c

2. Randall Flagg

3. Candice Moran

4. crème de menthe

5. three

6. 1644 80966

7. 108

8. Captain Tripps

9. Donald Merwin Elbert

10. A Gibson with a hand-rubbed cherry finish

11. Geraldo

12. Ogunquit

13. d

14. d

15. Caslin, Nebraska; 11/14/68

16. Russell Faraday

17. Project Blue

18. Brian Ball

19. a, b, c, d, e

20. "The First Noel"

5. THE DEAD ZONE

1. 55 months

2. Old Bear

3. b

4. Runaround Pond, Durham, Maine

5. He was a door-to-door Bible salesman

6. He commits suicide by cutting his own throat and hanging himself in the bathroom

7. March 4, 1978

8. Remington 700 .243 caliber rifle

9. WMTQ

10. $110

11. 5 mg

12. A 1957 Cadillac

13. John Smith

14. 43

15. Black Jack Pershing

16. He is an Amtrak conductor

17. b, c

18. Cleaves Mills Chevron

19. Black spots in John Smith's memory

20. c

6. FIRESTARTER

1. d

2. Lot Six

3. b

4. Pyrokinesis; "the bad thing"

5. Vickie Tomlinson

6. To a cottage at Tashmore Pond

7. What happens to people at the moment of death

8. d

9. e

10. John Rainbird

11. Telekinesis; Carrie White

12. Room 70, Jason Gearnigh Hall, Harrison College

13. Orville Jamieson

14. RASP or BROW

15. "Cancer of the credibility"

16. Telemyne Corp.

17. b

18. BIMBO

19. Dr. Joseph Wanless

20. A 1978 Vega; LMS 240

7. CUJO

1. b

2. Adworx

3. Twinkles; Sharp

4. Joe Cambers

5. Pinto

6. Red Razberry Zingers

7. Five years old; 200 pounds

8. Image-Eye

9. Thornton's Egg Farms

10. She beats him with a baseball bat

11. Trace Optical

12. True

13. Tadder

14. George Meara; he farts too much

15. Steve Kemp

16. Monsters stay out of this room! / You have no business here. / No monsters under Tad's bed! / You can't fit under there.

17. United Cerebral Palsy

18. Vermont Maid

19. c

20. His brother, David King

8. THE DARK TOWER I: THE GUNSLINGER

1. Michael Whalen

2. "The Man in Black fled across the desert and the Gunslinger followed. . . ."

3. *The Magazine of Fantasy & Science Fiction*

4. khef

5. bullets

6. David

7. Steel and nickel

8. Devil grass

9. A 1976 blue Cadillac

10. Slow Mutants

11. The Tower

12. He has aged ten years

13. The Beast

14. Maerlyn

15. Magic or enchantment

16. d

17. b, c, e

18. Walter

19. Zoltan

20. Three hamburgers and a beer

9. CHRISTINE

1. c

2. c

3. Carson Brothers; I0376 extension

4. Studio 2000

5. Mr. Thompson

6. 5'8"

7. Captain Beefheart; He was hit by a UPS truck

8. Darnell's Garage on Hampton Street

9. Randy Throgmorton

10. Sander Galton

11. A 1975 Duster

12. WDIC

13. George Romero

14. The Asshole Brigade

15. *Sketches of Love and Beauty*

16. The Ridge Rock Bears

17. A Camaro

18. 97,432.6

19. Barnswallow Drive

20. H & R Block

10. PET SEMATARY

1. He is head of University Medical Services at the University of Maine

2. The Wendigo

3. a

4. Church

5. He comes back to life

6. Almost 8000

7. A seven-room New England colonial

8. Judson Crandall; 83

9. Rheumatoid arthritis

10. Solitaire

11. Judd Crandall

12. $67,000

13. September 15, 1968

14. His father-in-law, Irwin Goldman

15. Surrendra Hardu

16. Steve Masterson

17. *The Magazine of College Medicine*

18. A 1917 Rolls Royce Silver Ghost

19. A Honda Civic

20. A Polaroid SX-70

11. CYCLE OF THE WEREWOLF

1. The twelve months of the year

2. Twelve monthly

3. e

4. He was a flagman on the GS & WM Railroad

5. He ripped his head off

6. Marty Coslaw

7. He ripped his back open

8. a, b, f

9. The Reverend Lester Lowe

10. Acute hypertension

11. Chris Wrightson

12. d

13. Nine sows and two boars

14. a, d, e

15. The left eye

16. A .38 caliber Colt Woodsman

17. Wright's Hill

18. Clyde Corliss, the werewolf's fifth victim; he is found gutted, hanging upside down over the church pulpit

19. d

20. Elise Fournier, Billy Robertson's bar maid

12. THE TALISMAN

1. c

2. Queen Laura

3. The Territories

4. Morgan is his dead father's Twinner in the Territories

5. Point Venuti, CA

6. The Heron Bar

7. Judge General

8. The Burger King in Daleville

9. Twelve

10. Traveling Jack

11. The Box

12. $4.10

13. c

14. A crystal globe, three feet in circumference

15. A Weatherbee .360 rifle

16. Magic Juice (wine)

17. Lily Cavanaugh

18. a, c, d, e

19. Ferd Janklow's

20. d

13. IT

1. The Derry, Maine, sewer system

2. 7 Seven

3. a, b, c, d, e

4. The South Windham Boys' Training Facility

5. He stutters

6. 207–941–8282

7. b

8. George Denbrough

9. Pennywise the Dancing Clown

10. Adrian Mellon

11. Ben Hascomb

12. c

13. Henry Bowers

14. Asthma

15. King & Landry

16. "The Dark"

17. "Come home, come home, come home"

18. $11,000 a year

19. c

20. c

14. THE EYES OF THE DRAGON

1. The Devil

2. The Napkins

3. For Naomi King

4. The Needle

5. Delain

6. They are brothers

7. Flagg

8. She choked on a lemon slice

9. Sasha of the Western Barony

10. Roland's penis

11. A remission of Taxes

12. Hunting

13. Fresh raw dragon heart

14. God and dog

15. Five

16. A dollhouse

17. Anna Crookbrow

18. Ben Staad

19. Lord High Groom

20. Peony

15. MISERY

1. Sidewinder, Colorado

2. Misery

3. n

4. *Misery's Return*

5. Misery Chastain

6. *Fast Cars*

7. The left

8. KTKA

9. A do-bee

10. He hits her with a typewriter and shoves a burning manuscript down her throat

11. Hastings House; Charles Merrill

12. Eddie Desmond

13. Eight

14. c

15. c, d

16. Dirty bird

17. A Flair Fine Liner

18. The Roydmans

19. 42

20. $506.17

16. THE TOMMYKNOCKERS

1. d

2. Haven, Maine

3. Peter, a beagle

4. The New England Paper Company

5. d

6. *Boxing the Compass*

7. Alice Kimball

8. It puts his cataract in active remission

9. Whopper Spareribs

10. Cutty Sark, double, water back

11. Delbert Chiles

12. The New England Poetry Caravan

13. Altair-4

14. Radio commercials for Sing's Polynesian restaurant

15. b, f

16. The Young Men for Christ

17. A force field

18. a, c

19. A Cessna Hawk KP

20. Route 9

17. THE DARK TOWER II: THE DRAWING OF THE THREE

1. "Child Roland to the Dark Tower Came"

2. He cuts off two fingers from his right hand and the big toe from his right foot

3. It has "moved on"

4. Marten

5. 37

6. Eddie Dean; heroine

7. .45 caliber

8. 1927

9. Keflex

10. Dead Right There

11. Jack Andolini; Old Double Ugly

12. 1964; She was pushed under a subway

13. The Wonderful Rambo Machine

14. c

15. "The Prisoner," a baboon

16. The Spics of Supremacy

17. Odetta Susannah Holmes, Detta Susannah Walter, and Susannah Dean

18. Teflon

19. Code 19

20. The Nice Notions counter at Macy's

18. THE DARK TOWER III: THE WASTE LANDS

1. Blaine; Topeka

2. "One made from many"

3. SHARDIK

4. Aunt Talitha

5. Apple beer

6. Oy

7. The Tick Tock Man

8. 800 mph

9. A cat has claws at the end of his paws; a complex sentence has a pause at the end of its clause

10. One is one's born kin; the other is a corn bin

11. 555–7661

12. 555–6712

13. The Manhattan Restaurant of the Mind

14. The Gunslinger is the Truth/Roland is the Truth/The Prisoner is the Truth/The Lady of Shadows is the Truth

15. A billy bumble

16. Mid-World

17. Rhinehold Street on Dutch Hill

18. Snow's Clam Fry-Ettes

19. Gasher

20. A Mark Cross pen

19. THE DARK HALF

1. George Stark

2. Alan Pangborn

3. c

4. May 23, 1988

5. "Not a very nice guy"

6. William and Wendy

7. Alexis Machine

8. A 1967 GMC pick-up; a black Toronado

9. Deke Bradford

10. A sparrow

11. 96529Q

12. A Scripto pen; A Berol Black Beauty

13. In a shin holster

14. Honors Course in Creative Writing (Eh-7A)

15. "Outside Marty's House"

16. Dr. Hugh Pritchard; a partially absorbed twin

17. Pokes his eye out with a paper clip

18. Colt Hi-Point loads

19. Rawlie DeLesseps

20. *Steel Machine*

20. NEEDFUL THINGS

1. Leland Gaunt

2. Polly Chalmers; arthritis

3. d

4. Our Lady of Serene Waters; The Mellow Tiger

5. a

6. A picture of Elvis Presley

7. Dick Perry Siding & Door Company

8. A lalique vase

9. Akron, Ohio

10. Danforth Keeton III

11. b

12. 5'6''; Barney

13. A Bazun lake-and-stream fishing rod

14. 800-EAT-SHIT

15. $17

16. Eddie Warburton

17. Carl Dorfman

18. Cobra

19. An azka or azakah

20. Ace Merrill

21. GERALD'S GAME

1. d

2. July 20, 1963

3. Kwashwakamak Lake

4. d

5. Gerald's penis

6. Catherine Sutlin

7. The shore of Dark Score Lake

8. Raymond Andrew Joubert

9. A wicker box

10. M-17s

11. Her father

12. Bill Green

13. Adrienne Gilette

14. The Goodwife

15. Dark Score Lake

16. Nora Callighan

17. "Some day my prince will tongue"

18. Homeland Cemetery

19. Megan Landis

20. White

22. DOLORES CLAIBORNE

1. d

2. Little Toll Island, Maine

3. Andy Bissette, Frank Proulx

4. Her husband, Joe St. George

5. c

6. A car accident near Baltimore

7. Sociable Security

8. Chip Freneau

9. d

10. His daughter Selina

11. She makes him fall down a well; the oaks

12. Dr. John McAuliffe; Scotland

13. c

14. d

15. Dust bunnies

16. Breaks her neck falling down the stairs

17. Sammy Marchant

18. Dolores's son, Joe Jr.

19. Spode

20. e

23. INSOMNIA

1. $27.95; 787 pages

2. The Red Apple

3. Cancer; Dr. Litchfield

4. Ralph's older friends

5. Ed Deepneau

6. Susan Day; *Lilies of the Valley*; battered women

7. Woman Care

8. b, d

9. The Maine LifeWatch Committee

10. Back Pages

11. Clotho; Lachesis

12. Atropos

13. "A woman needs a man like a fish needs a bicycle"

14. A pink triangle pin

15. Roland

16. Lois Chasse; Simone Castonguay

17. The Great Eastern Insurance Company

18. A hemorrhoid

19. Shorts; Dr. A

20. Helen Deepneau's daughter Natalie

24. ROSE MADDER

1. c

2. Seeing a single drop of blood on the bedsheets

3. "Service, Loyalty, Community"

4. A small bentwood rocking chair

5. Liberty City Loan & Pawn

6. Robert Leffert at the Tape Engine Studio

7. a

8. Rose Madder

9. With Bill Steiner

10. 897 Trenton Street, Liberty City

11. Pamela Gertrude Steiner; eight pounds, nine ounces

12. 251 Durham Avenue, Liberty City

13. Travelers Aid

14. She pees on him

15. Green and orange

16. The Hot Pot

17. Crickets

18. Biting himself and others

19. Tettinger's Pier

20. Marilyn Chambers

25. THE GREEN MILE

1. 6'8''; weight estimated to be between 280 and 350 pounds

2. Old Sparky

3. Mr. Jingles

4. The Cold Mountain Penitentiary, E Block; The Georgia Pines

5. Brad Dolan

6. c

7. Percy Wetmore; Brutus Howell

8. Melinda Moores, the warden's wife

9. Six

10. With Elaine Connelly

11. A swarm of black insects

12. A silver St. Christopher medallion

13. The University of Florida

14. 64; 104

15. Billy the Kid

16. d

17. Teflon

18. Percy Wetmore

19. The Resource Center

20. Burt Hammersmith

26. DESPERATION

1. "Death on the Second Shift"

2. A dead tiger-stripe cat

3. Rattlesnake #3 (known as the China Pit) in Desperation, Nevada

4. b

5. b

6. Tak

7. Jim Reed; Dave Pearson, and Collie Entragian

8. The Diablo Co.

9. a, e

10. c

11. Ini

12. e

13. Crocodile; $395

14. 248 Poplar Street, Wentworth, Ohio

15. *American Heart 1966–1996*

16. The Owl's Club; "Enjoy our Slotspitality"

17. Sarx

18. An ancient Earth spirit

19. They get taller

20. Prayboy

PART TWO: THE BACHMAN BOOKS

27. RAGE

1. *Getting It On*

2. Stephen King

3. Placerville H.S.

4. Ted Jones

5. Bangor, Maine

6. Thomaston State Prison

7. Charlie Decker; Jean Alice Underwood and John Downes Vance

8. "Self Integrity and a Normal Response to It"; *Seventeen* magazine

9. Sarah Pasterne

10. He's a textbook salesman

11. 6 left, 30 right, left to zero

12. Ted Jones's

13. Jerry Kesserling

14. Herk Orville

15. A green 1966 Pontiac

16. Frank Philbrick

17. Ted Jones

18. Judge Samuel K. N. Deleary

19. On the Mississippi Mud

20. Slitting a person's nose with a knife

28. THE LONG WALK

1. 167 lbs.; 160 lbs.

2. #3; #47; #61

3. The Major

4. Four miles per hour or faster; four

5. Conserve energy whenever possible

6. 7¾ miles

7. Slow and easy does it

8. Curley

9. Do not wear sneakers

10. Snappy Crackers

11. No interference with your fellow walkers

12. "I Rode the Mount Washington Cog Railway"

13. b

14. Tressler

15. Dom L'Antio

16. d

17. "Why do you feel qualified to participate in the Long Walk?"

18. May

19. Tubbins

20. Stebbins

29. ROADWORK

1. *A Novel of the First Energy Crisis*

2. Ammo Harvey's Gun Shop Ammo

3. WDST Weatherphone

4. 1241 Crestallen Street West; a split-level ranch house

5. 849–6330

6. *Facing the Lions* by Tom Wicker

7. Amoco

8. Player's Navy Cut cigarettes, medium

9. The 784 extension

10. $2000; 1 percent

11. b, c, d

12. Steve Ordner; a Delta 88

13. b

14. Brain tumor

15. Castleton

16. Southern Comfort and 7UP

17. The Andyburger

18. b, c

19. b, c

20. He works at Brite-Kleen as a maintenance man

30. THE RUNNING MAN

1. Arnold Schwarzenegger

2. Co-Op City

3. *Treadmill to Bucks*

4. Dokes; "Just the right temperature to stoke up a Doke—high to the nth degree"

5. 28; 6'2"; 165 lbs.; 126; XL

6. a, d

7. Rina Ward

8. (1)h (2)g (3)e (4)c (5)a (6)f (7)d (8)b

9. Assistant Director of Games

10. Engine wiper for General Atomics

11. Racial Act of 2004

12. b, c, d, e

13. Arthur Killian

14. Evan McCone; 30 days; $1 billion New Dollars

15. Steak, peas, mashed potatoes, milk, and apple cobbler with cream

16. *God as an Englishman; Not as a Stranger; The Pleasure of Serving*

17. Bobby Thompson; Fred Killian

18. c

19. A Lockheed Tristar Jet

20. A Silex

31. THINNER

1. The Good Luck Paint Company

2. Chamberlain Bridge

3. Susanne Lemke

4. It causes him to lose weight

5. Strawberry

6. Richard Ginelli

7. Flash

8. Frank Spurton

9. Brown University

10. The Henry Glassman Clinic

11. Bill Halleck's belly

12. Purfargade Ansiklet—"Child of the Night Flowers" in Rom

13. *Statistical Sociology*

14. Mexican brown heroin and strychnine

15. Judge Cary Rossington

16. A Kalishnikov AK-47 assault rifle

17. Bar Harbor, Maine

18. Lantern Drive, Fairview, CT

19. A Cadillac Cimarron

20. $687

32. THE REGULATORS

1. Montpelier, Vermont

2. Seth Garin

3. 1985; Claudia Inez Eschelman, his widow

4. The corner of Poplar and Hyacinth in Wentworth, Ohio; Cynthia Smith

5. John Marinville

6. An accounting firm

7. Cary Ripton

8. Veedon Brothers

9. c

10. *MotoKops 2200*

11. Pat the Kitty Cat

12. Hannibal; German shepherd

13. Nullo Impedimentum (no problem)

14. d

15. Adrian Givens

16. b

17. *The Force Corridor;* Allen Smithee

18. Electrical engineering

19. a, c, d, e

20. A giant gila monster

PART THREE: THE SHORT STORIES

33. NIGHT SHIFT

1. She discovers they're monsters

2. "Jerusalem's Lot"

3. "The Stand"

4. Jim Norman

5. $1.78 an hour

6. A6

7. Deep Space Antenna

8. Model-6 Speed Ironer and Folder

9. The bogeyman

10. Golden Light

11. c

12. The Morris Toy Company of Miami, Florida

13. Harold Davis High School; 3.88

14. Living With Literature

15. March 16, 1968

16. Marcia Cressner

17. 776–2390

18. 237 E. 46th Street, New York, NY

19. Public School 119, Bridgeport, CT

20. 5431

34. DIFFERENT SEASONS

1. "The Body"

2. 249B E. 35th Street, New York, NY

3. Waterhouse, Carden, Lawton, Frasier, and Effingham

4. "It is the tale; not he who tells it."

5. Edward Gray Seville

6. Thursday night

7. She delivers a baby after she is decapitated when struck by an auto

8. Dr. Emlyn McCarron

9. 30 years old; his wife, Linda Collins DeFresne

10. Glenn Quentin

11. a, b, c, d, e

12. Over $500

13. A pearl-handled razor; Diamond Pearl

14. $35,000

15. *The Santo Donato Clarion*

16. 963 Claremont Street; Kurt Dussander

17. A jar of quarters

18. *Greenspun Quarterly*, Fall 1970, Issue 45

19. Blueberry pie

20. $10,000

35. SKELETON CREW

1. Long Lake

2. Miss Kinney, Mrs. Trask, and Miss Bird

3. e

4. A .352 Magnum

5. c

6. Victor Carune; 1987

7. Maureen Romano

8. Cascade Lake

9. c

10. Henry Bowers

11. Fed Ship ASN/29

12. $250,000

13. Betsy Malenfant

14. He eats himself piece by piece

15. A Cresswell

16. Cramer's Dairy

17. 681–4330

18. Reg Thorpe

19. The Reach

20. Jonathan Hagstrom

36. FOUR PAST MIDNIGHT

1. b

2. The flight attendant waits until passengers have closed their eyes before asking them if they want anything

3. The Langoliers

4. A Polaroid Sun 660

5. Pop Merrill

6. Ardelia Lortz

7. American Pride Flight 29

8. She is blind

9. Ace

10. Nick Hopewell

11. Over forty

12. Representatives of Bankers International

13. The village of Fluting, England

14. Tashmore Lake; *The Organ-Grinders Boy*

15. Dellacourt, Mississippi

16. Ted Milner

17. Horseradish and Bermuda onion

18. Word Star 70 PC and word processor

19. 4:07 A.M. EST

20. He was a painter

37. NIGHTMARES & DREAMSCAPES

1. A Sedan DeVille

2. Dynamite wired to her car ignition explodes when she starts her car

3. 1121 Aster Drive, Hollywood Hills

4. Bow Wow

5. La Plata, Texas

6. b

7. A giant humanoid vampire bat

8. *Inside View*

9. Gloria Suet

10. Time

11. A stone fell off a gravel truck and hit his windshield, causing him to hit a telephone poll, where he was electrocuted by a wire

12. It rains a plague of killer toads

13. "The In-Migration of the French During the 17th Century"

14. d

15. Olga Katinya

16. e

17. b

18. Le Palais

19. Tabori Studios, studio F; *Beat It Till It's Dead*

20. Jory Hull

PART FOUR: MOVIES AND TV

38. STEPHEN KING AT THE MOVIES

1. e

2. Stanley Kubrick

3. Stephen King

4. c

5. Dee Wallace

6. Martin Sheen

7. Peter Horton

8. $1.8 million; $30 million

9. Linzi Hateley

10. Reggie Nalder; James Mason

11. Scatman Crothers

12. a, e

13. d

14. 25,000

15. Five

16. David Kronenberg; *An American Tragedy*

17. 23

18. *The Woman in the Room,* and *The Boogeyman*

19. Mark L. Lester

20. "Quitters, Inc.," "The Ledge," "The General"

21. *Cycle of the Werewolf*

22. Stephen King

23. *Stand by Me*

24. *Creepshow 2*

25. Richard Dawson

26. Fred Gwynne

27. b

28. *Stephen King's Graveyard Shift*

29. *Misery*

30. *Ghosts*

39. KING TV

1. 210 minutes; 1 hour

2. *Tales From the Darkside*

3. Harlan Ellison

4. William Widerman

5. *The Langoliers*

6. *It*

7. Harry Anderson

8. *Sometimes They Come Back*

9. He grows younger

10. *The Tommyknockers*

11. Gary Sinise

12. *The Stand*

13. Steven Weber

14. Tim Curry

15. Time rolls backward and minor earthquakes occur

16. *Golden Years*

17. Nicotine (he's a chain smoker)

18. Rebecca DeMornay

PART FIVE: STEPHEN KING, UP CLOSE AND PERSONAL

40. PROFESSIONAL LIFE

1. Wang; 1500 words every day of the year except Christmas, the Fourth of July, and his birthday, September 21

2. *Needful Things*

3. *The Shining, Misery*

4. *The Monster Squad* (The shirt is worn by the squad's leader, Sean Cranshaw.)

5. 6000

6. *Pet Sematary*

7. Fiction

8. Stephen King

9. *Desperation, The Regulators, The Green Mile*

10. More than 10,000

11. *The Shining*

12. Eric Norden

13. c

14. *Insomnia*

15. 1.5 million copies

16. d

17. More than 150 million

18. $40,000 plus a percentage of the gross

19. *The Magazine of Strange Stories;* $35

20. "Before the Play"

41. PERSONAL LIFE

1. 24

2. WZON; hard rock.

3. They are all 6'4"

4. Donald Spansky

5. a, b, c, d, f

6. Himself

7. Naomi, Joe, Owen

8. A night light

9. Vassar

10. Hampden Academy in Maine; about $6000 a year

11. Kings Garbage Truck

12. Lisbon High School in Lisbon Falls, Maine; 1966

13. c

14. a, b, c, d, e

15. a, b, c, d, e

16. Portland, Maine

17. *Tom Swift*

18. *Time* magazine for both

19. *Bluebook* and *Argosy*

20. d

42. TABITHA KING

1. Nodd's Ridge

2. The University of Maine at Orono

3. c

4. d

5. 29

6. Welsh corgi; Marlowe

7. Small World

8. Photographer

9. In college, at the University of Maine

10. Member, board of trustees

43. A POTPOURRI OF KING TRIVIA

1. More than 4 million

2. e (because "you plunge in")

3. d (because "everything's on the surface")

4. Half human, half cat

5. Ruth, Nevada

6. Ralph Vicananza

7. A free booklight; "It keeps you up at night"

8. Kathy Bates

9. Brad Leithauser

10. 14 years

11. Norman Daniels

12. Tabitha King

13. *Insomnia*

14. *A Simple Plan*; Scott Smith

15. $13 million

16. d

17. *Rolling Stone*

18. a, c, e

19. Stephen King

20. a, b, c, d, e, f

21. a, b, c, d, e

22. b, c, d, e

23. An accident

24. b

25. The Rock Bottom Remainders

26. New Line Cinema; $3.4 million

27. 22 rating, 34 share

28. Frank Darabont

29. "Lucky Quarter"

30. The Stanley Hotel, Estes Park, CO

44. A POTPOURRI OF KING TRIVIA, PART II

1. a, b, d, e

2. b

3. *'Salem's Lot*

4. e

5. *The House on Value Street*

6. *KnightRiders*

7. "The Way Station"

8. *Danse Macabre*

9. Uncle Clayton

10. Conquest

11. $60 a week

12. Harmone, Maine

13. Electrolux

14. His father's mother, Grandma Spansky

15. That one of his children will die

16. It is the tale; not he who tells it

17. b, e

18. c

19. The Moon Spinners

20. a, b, e

21. Writing screenplays of his stories and novels

22. "Do the Dead Sing?"

23. Donald M. Grant, Publisher

24. Courtland Mead

25. c

26. Consulting geologist for Diablo Mining

27. The entrance to a mine

28. Nevada Sunlite Entertainment

29. ANFO

30. Calf skin

45. A STEPHEN KING MISCELLANY

1. American Express

2. Edwin

3. The Boston Red Sox

4. "The Rats Are Loose on Flight 74"

5. He was raised Methodist

6. Seven years old

7. Richard Matheson

8. A hair dryer; $29

9. Family

10. Gary Hart

11. c

12. Triad Publishing Co.

13. e

14. January 2, 1971

15. *The Planet, Part 3: Heroes for Hope: Starring the X-Men*

16. a, b, c, d, f

17. b, c

18. c

19. The University of Maine

20. d

21. a, b, c, d, e

22. 1978

23. c, d

24. *My Pretty Pony;* $2200; the cover was made of steel

25. *Castle Rock*

26. *My Pretty Pony; Firestarter*

27. *True Tales of Demon Infestation*

28. Philtrum Press; *The Ideal, Genuine Man,* by Don Robertson

29. The Denebians

30. *Blaze*

31. Marcus Slade

32. Henry Coolidge; his niece, Kit Longtin

33. Clive Barnes

34. Dave Gardener

35. Bill Wallace

36. He owns an appliance store in New Hampshire

37. The moon was slow in the first quarter

38. Robert Ludlum

39. Stephen King

40. c

ABOUT THE AUTHOR

Bob Bly is the author of 100 magazine articles and more than 35 books, including *The Ultimate Unauthorized Star Trek Quiz Book* (HarperCollins) and *Comic Book Heroes: 1,001 Trivia Questions About America's Favorite Superheroes* (Carol Publishing Group). He has read every commercially published Stephen King book and is an avid fan.

Questions and comments on *The Ultimate Unauthorized Stephen King Trivia Challenge* may be sent to:

> Bob Bly
> 22 E. Quackenbush Avenue
> Dumont, NJ 07628
> e-mail: Rwbly@aol.com